BLOOM
Founded by | arihant

Olympiad ACE

A Comprehensive Practice Book

for School Olympiads & Talent Search Exams

GENERAL KNOWLEDGE

Class 10

by

Suman Bharti

Olympiad ACE

BLOOM

Bloom Cap Edu Ventures Pvt. Ltd.

卐 **Administrative & Production Office**

'Ramchhaya' 4577/15, Agarwal Road, Darya Ganj, New Delhi -110002
Tele: 011- 47630600, 43518550

卐 **PRICE:** ₹125.00

Published by Arihant Publications (I) Ltd.

For further information about the books log on to
www.bloomcap.org

Follow us on

Preface

"Future belongs to those Who prepares for it today"

School Olympiads are National & International level competitions conducted by different Government, Non-Government & Educational Organisations with the purpose of making the children ready to face competitive exams. The challenging Questions asked in Olympiads motivate them to learn more & more and bring out the best result with improved academic performance. The Awards & Scholarship offered by Olympiads motivate children to aspire & strive for doing better and emerge out to be the best.

GK Olympiads

GK is the knowledge of every aspect of the human life, which may or may not be the part of routine academic studies but very important for the overall personality development of the students. It is more or less connected with the attentiveness and awareness. There can be different domains of GK like; History, Geography, Polity, Culture, Discovery, Sports, Current Affairs etc.

GK Olympiads help students in understanding the importance of General Knowledge and updations about National & International Affairs in daily life.

'Bloom GK Olympiad Study Book Class 10' is a perfect resource to Study & Practice for Olympiad Exams and other National & State Level Talent Search Exams & Other Competitions.

Some Special Features of Bloom GK Olympiad Study Books are;

- Complete coverage of all the topics related to GK;. History, Geography, Environment, Polity, Science, Sports, etc.
- Chapterwise Exercises having different types of Objective Questions.
- Olympiad Pattern Practice Sets at the end.

This book is prepared by Expert Panel with the utmost care, still if you have any suggestions regarding its improvement then feel free to contact us at support@bloomcap.org. We will try to inculcate your suggestions in the further editions.

Contents

Chapter 01

Ancient History

MCQs 1 Mark Questions

1. Who is credited with the discovery of site of Harappa in 1921?
(a) Dayaram Sahni (b) John Marshall
(c) Mortimer Wheeler (d) B B Lal

2. Which is the largest Indus Valley Site discovered in India?
(a) Harappa
(b) Mohenjodaro
(c) Lothal
(d) Rakhigarhi

3. Which among the following was/were worshipped in Indus Valley Civilisation?
(a) Mother Goddess
(b) Pashupati Yogi
(c) Natural elements such as wind, fire
(d) All of the above

4. The local name of Mohenjodaro is ....
(a) mound of the living
(b) mound of the tree
(c) mound of the dead
(d) mound of the survivor

5. Identify the ruler who fought the Battle of Hydaspes against Porus.
(a) Darius
(b) Alexander the Great
(c) Cyrus
(d) Xerxes

6. Who among the following was the founder of Magadha Empire?
(a) Chandragupta Maurya
(b) Mahapadmananda
(c) Bimbisara
(d) Ajatashatru

7. Which Magadha King founded the capital of Pataliputra?
(a) Ajatashatru (b) Udayin
(c) Shishunaga (d) Bimbisara

8. Identify the language which is used by Ashoka in his inscriptions.
(a) Pali (b) Prakrit
(c) Sanskrit (d) Arabic

9. Choose the incorrectly matched pair.
(a) Rigveda – Book of Verses
(b) Atharvaveda – Book on Science and Astronomy
(c) Samveda – Book of Chants
(d) Yajurveda – Book of Sacrifices

10. Which of the following sacrifices/yagyas were performed by rulers in the later Vedic period?
(a) Rajasuya (b) Ashwamedha
(c) Vajapeya (d) All of these

11. Which of the following dynasties succeeded the Mauryas?
(a) Satavahanas (b) Sungas
(c) Yavanas (d) Pandya

12. Which among the following was the capital of Sungas?
(a) Rajgriha
(b) Pataliputra
(c) Taxila
(d) Vikramshila

13. Which of the following plays describes the story of Pushyamitra Shunga?
(a) Mudrarakshasa
(b) Devichandragupta
(c) Malavikagnimitram
(d) Mrichhakatika

14. Who among the following was the first king of Satavahana dynasty?
(a) Pushyamitra (b) Simuka
(c) Kanishka (d) Ashoka

15. Arrange the following rulers of the Gupta Empire in chronological order of their rule.
(a) Chandragupta I, Samudragupta, Vishnugupta
(b) Vishnugupta, Samudragupta, Chandragupta I
(c) Samudragupta, Chandragupta I, Vishnugupta
(d) Vishnugupta, Chandragupta I, Samudragupta

16. Name the Indian ruler, who was credited with the title of Indian Napoleon due to his military achievements.
(a) Gotamiputra Satakarni
(b) Samudragupta
(c) Chandragupta I
(d) Kanishka

17. The history of which of the following regions is collectively known as Tamilakam or Sangam Age?
(a) Kerala
(b) Tamil Nadu
(c) Parts of Sri Lanka
(d) All of the above

18. Complete the given analogy.
Cheras : Vanji : : Pandyas : ?
(a) Madurai (b) Puhar
(c) Uraiyur (d) Kanchi

19. Identify the correctly matched pair(s) regarding the state emblems of dynasties of Sangam Age.
(a) Carp – Pandyas
(b) Tiger – Cholas
(c) Bow – Cheras
(d) All of the above

20. Who among the following served as the Asthana Kavi or primary poet in the Court of Harshavardhana?
(a) Kalidasa (b) Banabhatta
(c) Amarasimha (d) Harisena

MCQs 2 Marks Questions

21. Read the following statements regarding Magadha Empire and choose the correct option.
I. Dhanananda was the last King of Magadha before the conquest of Chandragupta Maurya.
II. Chandragupta Maurya was assisted by Chanakya in the conquest of Magadha.
III. Rajgriha was the capital of Magadha Empire before the establishment of Pataliputra.

Codes
(a) I and II (b) II and III
(c) I and III (d) All of the above

22. Identify the personality from the description given below.
- He was appointed as the Governor of Ujjain/Avanti by Bindusara.
- During his lifetime, he fought only one battle i.e. Battle of Kalinga.

(a) Ajatashatru (b) Ashoka
(c) Samprati (d) Salisuka

23. Identify the ancient Indian Empire marked as A on the map given below which was founded by Pushyamitra.

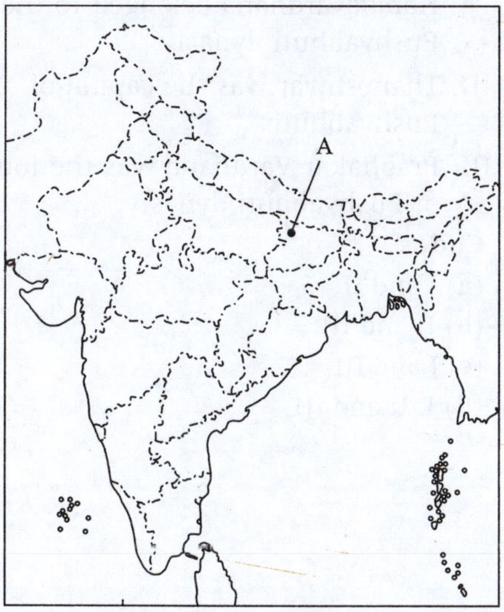

(a) Satavahana Empire (b) Sunga Empire
(c) Mauryan Empire (d) Gupta Empire

24. Read the following statements regarding Gupta Empire and identifies which ones are true (T) and which ones are false (F).

I. Founder of Gupta Empire was Sri Gupta.

II. Famous Chinese pilgrim, Fa-hien visited India, during the reign of Samudragupta.

III. Kumaragupta founded Nalanda University.

IV. Allahabad Pillar inscription describes the achievements and qualities of Chandragupta I.

Codes

	I	II	III	IV
(a)	T	T	T	T
(b)	F	F	F	F
(c)	T	F	T	F
(d)	T	F	F	F

25. Read the following statements and choose the correct option.

I. Sangam period is known as the 'classical age' of the Tamils.

II. During the Sangam age, Tamil region was ruled by Cholas, Chera and Pandyas Dynasties.

Codes

(a) Only I
(b) Only II
(c) Both I and II
(d) None of the above

26. Match the following.

	List I (Towns)		List II (Discoveries)
A.	Harappa	1.	Granaries
B.	Mohenjodaro	2.	Bronze Dancing Girl Statue
C.	Lothal	3.	Artificial dockyard
D.	Rakhigarhi	4.	Production of terracotta

Codes

	A	B	C	D
(a)	1	2	3	4
(b)	2	1	3	4
(c)	4	3	2	1
(d)	3	4	1	2

27. There are two statements marked as Assertion (A) and Reason (R). Mark your answer as per the codes given below.

Assertion (A) Founder of Magadha was Jarasandha and Brihadratha.

Reason (R) Magadha was the most powerful and prosperous kingdom of North India in 6th century.

Codes

(a) Both A and R are true and R is the correct explanation of A

(b) Both A and R are true, but R is not the correct explanation of A

(c) A is true, but R is false

(d) A is false, but R is true

28. Read the following statements regarding Harshavardhana and choose the correct option.

I. Harshavardhana belonged to the Pushyabhuti dynasty.

II. Thaneshwar was the capital of Pushyabhutis.

III. Prabhakar Vardhana was the founder of Pushyabhuti dynasty.

Codes

(a) I and II

(b) II and III

(c) I and III

(d) I, II and III

Darken your choice with HB Pencil

1.	ⓐ ⓑ ⓒ ⓓ	6.	ⓐ ⓑ ⓒ ⓓ	11.	ⓐ ⓑ ⓒ ⓓ	16.	ⓐ ⓑ ⓒ ⓓ	21.	ⓐ ⓑ ⓒ ⓓ	26.	ⓐ ⓑ ⓒ ⓓ
2.	ⓐ ⓑ ⓒ ⓓ	7.	ⓐ ⓑ ⓒ ⓓ	12.	ⓐ ⓑ ⓒ ⓓ	17.	ⓐ ⓑ ⓒ ⓓ	22.	ⓐ ⓑ ⓒ ⓓ	27.	ⓐ ⓑ ⓒ ⓓ
3.	ⓐ ⓑ ⓒ ⓓ	8.	ⓐ ⓑ ⓒ ⓓ	13.	ⓐ ⓑ ⓒ ⓓ	18.	ⓐ ⓑ ⓒ ⓓ	23.	ⓐ ⓑ ⓒ ⓓ	28.	ⓐ ⓑ ⓒ ⓓ
4.	ⓐ ⓑ ⓒ ⓓ	9.	ⓐ ⓑ ⓒ ⓓ	14.	ⓐ ⓑ ⓒ ⓓ	19.	ⓐ ⓑ ⓒ ⓓ	24.	ⓐ ⓑ ⓒ ⓓ		
5.	ⓐ ⓑ ⓒ ⓓ	10.	ⓐ ⓑ ⓒ ⓓ	15.	ⓐ ⓑ ⓒ ⓓ	20.	ⓐ ⓑ ⓒ ⓓ	25.	ⓐ ⓑ ⓒ ⓓ		

Chapter 02

Medieval History

MCQs 1 Mark Questions

1. Prithviraj Raso written by Chandbardai provides valuable information about which dynasty?
(a) Cholas (b) Cheras
(c) Pandyas (d) Pratiharas

2. Which famous temple was attacked by Mahmud Ghazni in 1025 AD?
(a) Somnath Temple
(b) Jagannath Puri Temple
(c) Kedarnath Temple
(d) Dwarkadhish Temple

3. Identify the author of Kitab-ul-Hind who was also the court poet of Mahmud Ghaznavi.
(a) Al Biruni (b) Al Masudi
(c) Ibn Battuta (d) Abul Fazl

4. In the Second Battle of Tarain, Prithviraj Chauhan was defeated by which foreign invader?
(a) Muhammad Ghori
(b) Ghiyas-ud din Muhammad
(c) Muizzudin Muhammad
(d) Qutub-ud-Din Aibak

5. Complete the given analogy
Solankis : Gujarat : : Chauhans : ?
(a) Rajasthan (b) Karnataka
(c) Tamil Nadu (d) Kerala

6. Choose the incorrectly matched pair.

Dynasty		Rulers
(a) Slave Dynasty	–	Iltutmish
(b) Lodi Dynasty	–	Jalauddin
(c) Khalji Dynasty	–	Alauddin
(d) Tughlaq Dynasty	–	Muhammad Bin

7. Which ruler of Delhi Sultanate completed the construction of Qutub Minar?
(a) Qutub-ud-Din Aibak
(b) Iltutmish
(c) Alauddin Khalji
(d) Ibrahim Lodi

8. Who was the first and the only woman ruler of Delhi Sultanate?
(a) Razia Sultan (b) Mehrunissa
(c) Nur Jahan (d) Gulbadan Begum

9. Which Delhi Sultanate ruler is credited with the construction of Alai Darwaza?
(a) Jalaluddin Khalji (b) Alauddin Khalji
(c) Iltutmish (d) Sikandar Lodi

10. Identify the official language of Delhi Sultanate.
(a) Arabic (b) Persian
(c) Urdu (d) Hindawi

11. Which ruler is credited with the construction of Agra City?
(a) Sikandar Lodi (b) Ibrahim Lodi
(c) Bahlul Lodi (d) Balban

12. Choose the correctly matched pair regarding the battles fought by Babur with various rulers.
(a) Battle of Khanwa – Rana Sanga
(b) Battle of Chanderi – Medini Rai
(c) Battle of Ghaghra – Mohammad Lodi
(d) All of the above

13. Identify the ruler who was defeated by the army of Akbar in the Battle of Haldighati.
(a) Rana Sanga (b) Maharana Udai Singh
(c) Amar Singh (d) Maharana Pratap

14. Who was defeated by Akbar in the Second Battle of Panipat in 1556?
(a) Hemu (b) Sher Shah Suri
(c) Maharana Pratap (d) Muhammad Ghori

15. Identify the town that was established by Mughal ruler Akbar.
(a) Agra (b) Delhi
(c) Lahore (d) Fatehpur Sikri

16. Which Mughal ruler adopted the title of Nur-ud-din?
(a) Jahangir (b) Shah Jahan
(c) Aurangzeb (d) Akbar

17. Name the foreign traveller(s) who visited India during Vijayanagara Empire.
(a) Nicolo Di Conti (b) Abdur Razzaq
(c) Domingo Paes (d) All of these

18. The founders of Vijayanagara Empire belonged to which dynasty?
(a) Tuluva Dynasty (b) Sangam Dynasty
(c) Aravidu Dynasty (d) Saluva Dynasty

19. Which Maratha ruler was the contemporary rival of Aurangzeb?
(a) Chhatrapati Shivaji Maharaj
(b) Shahaji Raje Bhonsle
(c) Balaji Baji Rao
(d) Shahu Maharaj

20. During the Chhatrapati Shivaji Maharaj rule, what was the capital of Maratha kingdom?
(a) Pune (b) Raigarh
(c) Karwar (d) Purandhar

21. Who among the following was the first Peshwa under Peshwai of Maratha Empire in 18th Century?
(a) Balaji Baji Rao (b) Balaji Vishwanath
(c) Shahu Maharaj (d) Raghoba Dada

MCQs 2 Marks Questions

22. Read the following statements and identifies which ones are true (T) and which ones are false (F).
I. Aurangzeb assumed the title Alamgir.
II. Ibrahim Lodi was the last ruler of Delhi Sultanate.
III. Shah Jahan transferred the capital of Mughal Empire to Delhi from Agra.

Codes

	I	II	III		I	II	III
(a)	T	T	T	(b)	F	F	F
(c)	T	F	T	(d)	F	T	F

23. There are two statements marked as Assertion (A) and Reason (R). Mark your answer as per the codes given below.
Assertion (A) Babur won the first Battle of Panipat.
Reason (R) Babur was the first to introduce the use of cannons in India.
Codes
(a) Both A and R are true and R is the correct explanation of A
(b) Both A and R are true, but R is not the correct explanation of A
(c) A is true, but R is false
(d) A is false, but R is true

24. Identify the personality from the description given below.
• He was also known as Andhra Bhoja.

- He belonged to Tuluva Dynasty of Vijayanagara Empire.

(a) Krishnadeva Raya (b) Sri Ranga III
(c) Deva Raya 1 (d) Deva Raya II

25. Refer to the marking in the following map. Which ruler of Delhi Sultanate shifted his capital from Lahore to the region marked in the given map?

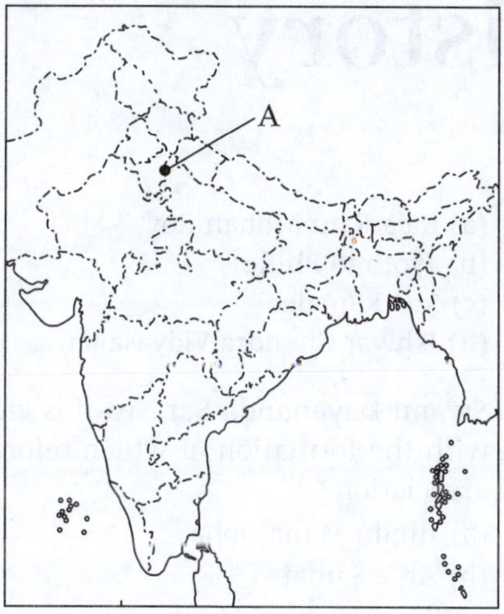

(a) Iltutmish
(b) Qutub-ud-Din Aibak
(c) Sikandar Lodi
(d) Ibrahim Lodi

26. Match the following.

List I (Monuments)	**List II** (Associated Ruler)
A. Char Minar	1. Mohammed Quli Qutb Shah
B. Buland Darwaza	2. Qutub-ud-Din Aibak
C. Adhai Din ka Jhonpra	3. Akbar

Codes

	A	B	C
(a)	3	2	1
(b)	1	3	2
(c)	2	1	3
(d)	3	1	2

Darken your choice with HB Pencil

1. ⓐ ⓑ ⓒ ⓓ	6. ⓐ ⓑ ⓒ ⓓ	11. ⓐ ⓑ ⓒ ⓓ	16. ⓐ ⓑ ⓒ ⓓ	21. ⓐ ⓑ ⓒ ⓓ	26. ⓐ ⓑ ⓒ ⓓ
2. ⓐ ⓑ ⓒ ⓓ	7. ⓐ ⓑ ⓒ ⓓ	12. ⓐ ⓑ ⓒ ⓓ	17. ⓐ ⓑ ⓒ ⓓ	22. ⓐ ⓑ ⓒ ⓓ	
3. ⓐ ⓑ ⓒ ⓓ	8. ⓐ ⓑ ⓒ ⓓ	13. ⓐ ⓑ ⓒ ⓓ	18. ⓐ ⓑ ⓒ ⓓ	23. ⓐ ⓑ ⓒ ⓓ	
4. ⓐ ⓑ ⓒ ⓓ	9. ⓐ ⓑ ⓒ ⓓ	14. ⓐ ⓑ ⓒ ⓓ	19. ⓐ ⓑ ⓒ ⓓ	24. ⓐ ⓑ ⓒ ⓓ	
5. ⓐ ⓑ ⓒ ⓓ	10. ⓐ ⓑ ⓒ ⓓ	15. ⓐ ⓑ ⓒ ⓓ	20. ⓐ ⓑ ⓒ ⓓ	25. ⓐ ⓑ ⓒ ⓓ	

Chapter 03

Modern History

MCQs 1 Mark Questions

1. Which Governor General of India introduced the policy of Doctrine of Lapse?
(a) Lord Dalhousie (b) Lord Bentinck
(c) Lord Hastings (d) Lord Amherst

2. Who was the Governor General of India during the Revolt of 1857?
(a) Lord Dalhousie
(b) Lord Canning
(c) Lord Irwin
(d) Lord Linlithgow

3. Identify the personality/personalities who were associated with the Revolt of 1857.
(a) Mangal Pandey
(b) Bahadur Shah Zafar
(c) Veer Kunwar Singh
(d) All of the above

4. Which Indian Nationalist referred to Revolt of 1857 as First War of Independence?
(a) V D Savarkar
(b) Bal Gangadhar Tilak
(c) Bhagat Singh
(d) Mangal Pandey

5. Who was considered as the first Modern Man as well as Father of Indian Renaissance?
(a) Raja Ram Mohan Roy
(b) Jyotirao Phule
(c) MG Ranade
(d) Ishwar Chandra Vidyasagar

6. Swami Dayananda Saraswati is credited with the formation of which reform association?
(a) Hindu Mahasabha
(b) Arya Samaj
(c) Young Bengal Movement
(d) Prarthana Samaj

7. Who among the following played an active role in foundation of Indian National Congress?
(a) AO Hume
(b) Dadabhai Naoroji
(c) Bal Gangadhar Tilak
(d) Lala Lajpat Rai

8. Where did the first session of Indian National Congress take place?
(a) Bombay (b) Calcutta
(c) Madras (d) Lahore

9. Identify the personality, who is known as the Unofficial Ambassador of India.
(a) Dadabhai Naoroji
(b) Syed Ahmed Khan
(c) Lala Lajpat Rai
(d) Gopal Krishna Gokhale

10. Identify the first President of Indian National Congress who is shown in the image given below.

(a) Dadabhai Naoroji
(b) Womesh Chandra Banerjee
(c) AO Hume
(d) Annie Besant

11. .... is regarded as Mahatma Gandhi's political guru.
(a) Gopal Krishna Gokhale
(b) Surendranath Banerjee
(c) Bal Gangadhar Tilak
(d) A O Hume

12. Complete the given analogy.
Moderate leader : Dadabhai Naoroji : : Extremist leader : ?
(a) Bipin Chandra Pal
(b) Gopal Krishna Gokhale
(c) Surendranath Banerjee
(d) Womesh Chandra Banerjee

13. National Song of India, Vande Mataram was first sung during which movement?
(a) Swadeshi Movement
(b) Non-Cooperation Movement
(c) Civil Disobedience Movement
(d) Quit India Movement

14. Where was Muslim League founded in 1906?
(a) Lahore (b) Madras
(c) Dhaka (d) Awadh

15. .... was appointed as the first honorary President of the Muslim League.
(a) MA Jinnah
(b) Aga Khan III
(c) Sir Syed Ahmed Khan
(d) Maulana Azad

16. In which session of Indian National Congress, Congress was splitted into Moderates and Extremists?
(a) Nagpur Session
(b) Calcutta session
(c) Lucknow Session
(d) Surat Session

17. Identify the leader(s) who was/were associated with the Home Rule Movement in India.
(a) Bal Gangadhar Tilak
(b) Annie Besant
(c) Mahatma Gandhi
(d) Both (a) and (b)

18. Choose the correctly matched pair.
(a) Champaran Satyagraha – Indigo planters
(b) Ahmedabad Satyagraha – Textile mill workers strike
(c) Kheda Satyagraha – Remittance of land revenue of peasants
(d) All of the above

19. Jallianwala Bagh Massacre was the consequence of which among the following?
(a) Rowlatt Act
(b) Morley Minto Reforms
(c) Partition of Bengal
(d) Chauri Chaura incident

20. Hunter Commission was appointed in India after which incidence?
(a) Dandi March
(b) Famines
(c) Chauri Chaura
(d) Jallianwala Bagh Massacre

21. Choose the activity/activities that was/were undertaken under Non-Cooperation Movement.

(a) Boycott of schools
(b) Boycott of law courts
(c) Picketting of shops selling foreign goods
(d) All of the above

22. What was the purpose of appointment of Simon Commission?

(a) To introduce Constitutional reforms
(b) To grant independence of India
(c) To frame a Constitution for India
(d) Both (b) and (c)

23. Poona Pact of 1931 took place between Mahatma Gandhi and ....

(a) BR Ambedkar
(b) Sardar Patel
(c) Jawaharlal Nehru
(d) Lord Irwin

24. Identify the leader(s) who was/were associated with Indian National Army.

(a) Mohan Singh
(b) Subhash Chandra Bose
(c) Rash Behari Bose
(d) All of the above

25. Who was the Governor General of India when India gained independence?

(a) Lord Irwin
(b) Lord Linlithgow
(c) Lord Mountbatten
(d) Lord Minto

MCQs 2 Marks Questions

26. Consider the following statements and choose the correct option.

I. Partition of Bengal took place in 1905.
II. Lord Curzon was the Governor General during the Partition of Bengal.
III. Mahatma Gandhi launched Swadeshi Movement after Partition of Bengal.

Codes

(a) I and II (b) II and III
(c) I and III (d) I, II and III

27. Consider the following statements and choose the correct option.

I. The Railways in India were introduced during the Governorship of Lord Dalhousie.
II. First railway line was established from Bombay to Thane.

Codes

(a) Only I (b) Only II
(c) Both I and II (d) None of these

28.

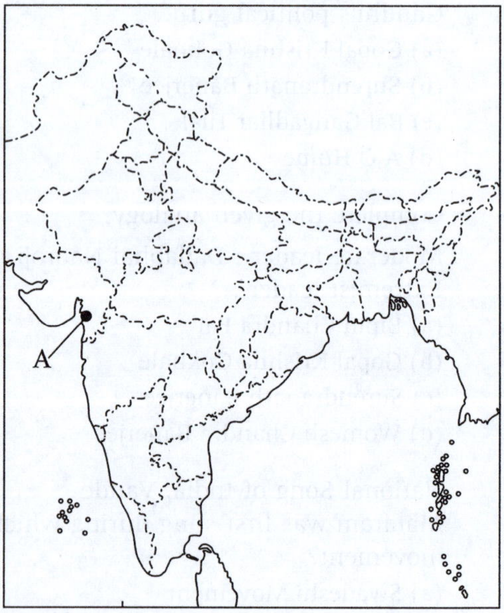

Refer to the marking in the above map and identify the region from where Gandhiji broke the Salt Law.

(a) Dandi (b) Amritsar
(c) Bombay (d) Sabarmati

29. Identify the Indian National Movement with the help of the information given below.

- This movement was launched due to the failure of Cripps Mission.
- It is also known as the Bharat Chhodo Andolan, launched at the Bombay Session of the All India Congress Committee.

(a) Civil Disobedience Movement

(b) Quit India Movement

(c) Swadeshi Movement

(d) Non-Cooperation Movement

30. There are two statements, marked as Assertion (A) and Reason (R). Mark your answer as per the codes given below.

Assertion (A) The Battle of Plassey was a war fought between the British East India Company and the Nawab of Bengal.

Reason (R) Battle of Plassey led to the consolidation of the British power in Bengal

Codes

(a) Both A and R are true and R is the correct explanation of A

(b) Both A and R are true, but R is not the correct explanation of A

(c) A is true, but R is false

(d) A is false, but R is true

Darken your choice with HB Pencil

1.	ⓐ ⓑ ⓒ ⓓ	6.	ⓐ ⓑ ⓒ ⓓ	11.	ⓐ ⓑ ⓒ ⓓ	16.	ⓐ ⓑ ⓒ ⓓ	21.	ⓐ ⓑ ⓒ ⓓ	26.	ⓐ ⓑ ⓒ ⓓ
2.	ⓐ ⓑ ⓒ ⓓ	7.	ⓐ ⓑ ⓒ ⓓ	12.	ⓐ ⓑ ⓒ ⓓ	17.	ⓐ ⓑ ⓒ ⓓ	22.	ⓐ ⓑ ⓒ ⓓ	27.	ⓐ ⓑ ⓒ ⓓ
3.	ⓐ ⓑ ⓒ ⓓ	8.	ⓐ ⓑ ⓒ ⓓ	13.	ⓐ ⓑ ⓒ ⓓ	18.	ⓐ ⓑ ⓒ ⓓ	23.	ⓐ ⓑ ⓒ ⓓ	28.	ⓐ ⓑ ⓒ ⓓ
4.	ⓐ ⓑ ⓒ ⓓ	9.	ⓐ ⓑ ⓒ ⓓ	14.	ⓐ ⓑ ⓒ ⓓ	19.	ⓐ ⓑ ⓒ ⓓ	24.	ⓐ ⓑ ⓒ ⓓ	29.	ⓐ ⓑ ⓒ ⓓ
5.	ⓐ ⓑ ⓒ ⓓ	10.	ⓐ ⓑ ⓒ ⓓ	15.	ⓐ ⓑ ⓒ ⓓ	20.	ⓐ ⓑ ⓒ ⓓ	25.	ⓐ ⓑ ⓒ ⓓ	30.	ⓐ ⓑ ⓒ ⓓ

Chapter 04

History of the World

MCQs 1 Mark Questions

1. Egyptian Civilisation flourished on the banks of .... river.
(a) Tigris (b) Euphrates
(c) Nile (d) Indus

2. Who among the following were first to evolve proper script of writing?
(a) Chinese (b) Sumerians
(c) Egyptians (d) Harappans

3. Which among the following were the cities in Greek Civilisation?
(a) Sparta (b) Athens
(c) Macedonia (d) All of these

4. Identify the country from where the Industrial Revolution began for the first time.
(a) US (b) UK
(c) France (d) Italy

5. Choose the correctly matched pair(s).

	Inventors		Inventions
(a)	James Hargreaves	–	Spinning Jenny
(b)	Richard Arkwright	–	Water Frame
(c)	James Watt	–	Steam Engine
(d)	All of the above		

6. The event of Boston Tea party is associated with which of the following?
(a) French Revolution
(b) American Revolution
(c) Industrial Revolution
(d) Unification of Germany

7. Who is the author of Declaration of Independence during American Revolution?
(a) Thomas Jefferson
(b) Bill Clinton
(c) George Washington
(d) John Adams

8. Who was elected as the first President of USA after the American Revolution?
(a) Bill Clinton
(b) George Washington
(c) George Bush
(d) Franklin Roosevelt

9. Which of the following ideas was/were promoted during the French Revolution of 1785?
(a) Liberty
(b) Equality
(c) Fraternity
(d) All of the above

10. Napoleonic Code of France was related to which among the following?
(a) Abolition of privileges based on birth
(b) Establishment of equality before law
(c) Secured right to property
(d) All of the above

11. The Kingdom of Sardinia was most powerful kingdom in which country?
(a) France
(b) Italy
(c) Russia
(d) Germany

12. Who among the following was/were the leaders of Young Italy Movement during the Unification of Italy?
(a) Mazzini
(b) Garibaldi
(c) Otto von Bismarck
(d) Both (a) and (b)

13. Which among the following was the most powerful Kingdom in Germany?
(a) Prussia (b) Sardinia
(c) Austria (d) Vienna

14. Identify the personality shown in the picturem, who played a leading role in Unification of Germany.

(a) Otto von Bismarck
(b) Kaisar William I
(c) Duke Metternich
(d) Fidel Castro

15. Identify the policy adopted by Otto Von Bismarck during the Unification of Germany.
(a) Blood and Iron (b) Carrot and Stick
(c) Iron Curtain (d) Blood and Sword

16. Complete the given analogy.
Central Powers : ? : : Allied Powers : France
(a) Germany (b) Japan
(c) USSR (d) Romania

17. What was the main cause of World War I?
(a) French Revolution
(b) Anglo French Rivalry
(c) Unification of Germany
(d) Colonisation

18. Identify the treaty that was concluded after World War I.
(a) Treaty of Versailles
(b) Treaty of Constantinople
(c) Peace of Westphalia
(d) Treaty of Paris

19. Name the organisation that was established after World War I.
(a) WTO
(b) United Nations
(c) League of Nations
(d) IMF

20. During the Russian Revolution, Bolshevik state was formed under the leadership of ....
(a) Fidel Castro
(b) Vladimir Lenin
(c) Garibaldi
(d) Lloyd George

21. Who is the author of the book 'The Communist Manifesto'?
(a) Karl Marx
(b) Lenin
(c) Sun Yat-sen
(d) Chiang Kai-shek

22. Identify the country that was previously known as Sickman of Europe.

(a) Turkey (b) Italy
(c) France (d) China

23. Who among the following was/were the part of Allied powers during World War II?

(a) Great Britain
(b) France
(c) USSR
(d) All of the above

24. Arrange the following events in chronological order.

(a) French Revolution, Chinese Revolution, Turkish Revolution
(b) Chinese Revolution, French Revolution, Turkish Revolution
(c) Turkish Revolution, Chinese Revolution, French Revolution
(d) Turkish Revolution, French Revolution, Chinese Revolution

MCQs 2 Marks Questions

25. Consider the following statements regarding Egyptian Civilisation and choose the correct option.

I. Egypt is called the Gift of Nile.
II. The Egyptian King was called Pharoh.
III. Pyramids and Sphinx were two specimens of Egyptian architectural excellence.

Codes

(a) I and II (b) II and III
(c) I and III (d) I, II and III

26. Identify the personality from the description given below

- He was the first European to visit China.
- He was Venetian Traveler and travelled from Venice to China and Japan.

(a) Marco Polo
(b) Columbus
(c) Prince Henry
(d) Magellan

27. Consider the following statements and choose the correct option.

I. 16th Century was commonly known as Age of Renaissance and Revival of Learning.
II. Glorious Revolution or Bloodless Revolution took place in England.

Codes

(a) Only I (b) Only II
(c) Both I and III (d) None of these

28.

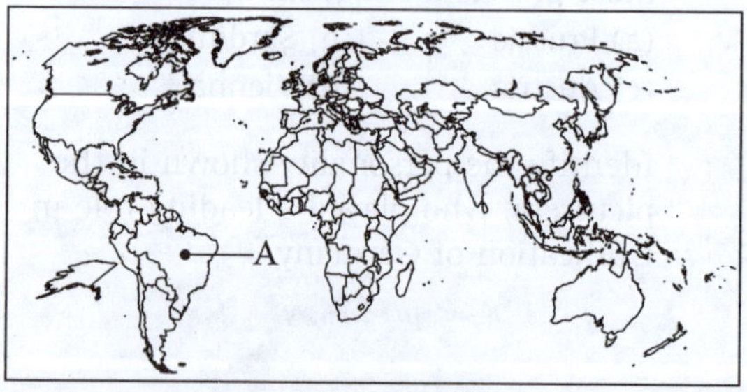

Refer to the marking (A) in the world map above and identify the country which was an Allied Power.

(a) Brazil (b) China
(c) Japan (d) Italy

29. Read the following statements and identifies which ones are true (T) and which ones are false (F).

I. Weimar Republic was the Constitution of Germany.

II. Germany under the Leadership of Hitler emerged victorious in World War II.

III. Weimar Republic was adopted by Adolf Hitler.

IV. There was democracy in Germany during the Rule of Hitler.

Codes

	I	II	III	IV		I	II	III	IV
(a)	F	F	F	F	(b)	T	T	T	T
(c)	F	T	F	T	(d)	T	F	F	F

30. Read the following statements and choose the correct option.

I. Mesopotamian Civilisation is the oldest civilisation in the world.

II. The Industrial Revolution first started in france.

III. Herodotus is known as the father of History.

Codes

(a) Only I

(b) Only II

(c) II and III

(d) I and III

Darken your choice with HB Pencil

1.	a	b	c	d	6.	a	b	c	d	11.	a	b	c	d	16.	a	b	c	d	21.	a	b	c	d	26.	a	b	c	d
2.	a	b	c	d	7.	a	b	c	d	12.	a	b	c	d	17.	a	b	c	d	22.	a	b	c	d	27.	a	b	c	d
3.	a	b	c	d	8.	a	b	c	d	13.	a	b	c	d	18.	a	b	c	d	23.	a	b	c	d	28.	a	b	c	d
4.	a	b	c	d	9.	a	b	c	d	14.	a	b	c	d	19.	a	b	c	d	24.	a	b	c	d	29.	a	b	c	d
5.	a	b	c	d	10.	a	b	c	d	15.	a	b	c	d	20.	a	b	c	d	25.	a	b	c	d	30.	a	b	c	d

Chapter 05

Art and Culture

MCQs 1 Mark Questions

1. Identify the ruler who is credited with the construction of Sanchi Stupa.
(a) Ashoka (b) Bindusara
(c) Bimbisara (d) Chandragupta Maurya

2. Kailashnath Temple is located in which caves?
(a) Ajanta Caves (b) Ellora Caves
(c) Karle Caves (d) Kanheri Caves

3. Who among the following are the pioneers of Dravidan style of temple architecture?
(a) Pallavas (b) Cholas
(c) Satavahanas (d) Chalukyas

4. Identify the temple(s) that was/were constructed according to Dravidan style of architecture.
(a) Shiva Temple, Thanjavur
(b) Meenakshi Temple, Tamil Nadu
(c) Kailashnath Temple, Ellora
(d) All of the above

5. Which among the following temples of India is known as Black Pagoda?
(a) Brihadeshwara Temple, Tanjore
(b) Sun Temple, Konark
(c) Lord Jagannath Temple, Puri
(d) Meenakshi Temple, Madurai

6. Name the ruler who is credited with the construction of Alai Darwaza and Hauz Khas in Delhi.
(a) Alauddin Khalji
(b) Iltutmish
(c) Akbar
(d) Firoz Shah Tughlaq

7. The given below picture depicts of Buland Darwaza. Identify the ruler who is credited with the construction of this architecture.

(a) Akbar (b) Shah Jahan
(c) Jahangir (d) Aurangzeb

8. Who is credited with the construction of Akbar's Tomb in Sikandra?
(a) Jahangir
(b) Shah Jahan
(c) Mariam-uz-Zamani
(d) Gulbadan Begum

9. The given picture is of Jama Masjid in Old Delhi. Identify the ruler who is credited with the construction of Jama Masjid.

(a) Jahangir (b) Shah Jahan
(c) Akbar (d) Aurangzeb

10. The statue of Dancing Girl and Pashupati Seal are associated with which civilisation?
(a) Egyptian Civilisation
(b) Mesopotamian Civilisation
(c) Greek Civilisation
(d) Harappan Civilisation

11. Complete the given analogy.
Mathura School of Sculpture : Kushanas : : Amravati School of Sculpture : ?
(a) Chalukyas (b) Pallavas
(c) Satavahanas (d) Cholas

12. Who among the following established 'Indian Society of Oriental Art'?
(a) Rabindranath Tagore
(b) Abanindranath Tagore
(c) Satyajit Ray
(d) Raja Ravi Varma

13. Kalighat Painting style originated in which Indian state?
(a) Bihar (b) Odisha
(c) West Bengal (d) Karnataka

14. Choose the correctly matched pair.
(a) Kalamkari Painting – Andhra Pradesh
(b) Warli Painting – Maharashtra
(c) Madhubani Painting – Bihar
(d) All of the above

15. Identify the type of painting which is depicted in the image given below.

(a) Madhubani (b) Kalamkari
(c) Warli (d) Kalighat Painting

16. Which of the following Akademis is responsible for fostering the development of dance, drama and music in India?
(a) National School of Drama
(b) Sangeet Akademi
(c) Sahitya Akademi
(d) Lalit Kala Akademi

17. Which among the following festivals is/are celebrated during the harvesting season?
(a) Baisakhi (b) Bihu
(c) Onam (d) All of these

18. Choose the incorrectly matched pair
(a) Pongal – Tamil Nadu
(b) Onam – Kerala
(c) Kambala – Bihar
(d) Baisakhi – Punjab

19. Gudi Padwa is a traditional festival of which Indian state?
(a) Uttar Pradesh (b) Gujarat
(c) Maharashtra (d) Odisha

MCQs 2 Marks Questions

20. Match the following.

	List I		List II
A.	Kuchipudi	1.	Andhra Pradesh
B.	Mohiniyattam	2.	Kerala
C.	Chhau	3.	Jharkhand
D.	Lavani	4.	Maharashtra

Codes

	A	B	C	D		A	B	C	D
(a)	1	2	3	4	(b)	2	1	4	3
(c)	3	4	2	1	(d)	4	3	1	2

21. Consider the following statements regarding languages and choose the incorrect option.

I. There are 22 official languages in Indian Constitution.

II. Hindi is not the official language of India.

III. Hindi is the National Language of India.

Codes

(a) I and II (b) II and III
(c) I and III (d) I, II and III

22. There are two statements marked as Assertion (A) and Reason (R). Mark your answer as per the codes given below.

Assertion (A) Virupaksha Temple is located at Hampi, Karnataka.

Reason (R) Hampi was the capital of Vijayanagara Empire.

Codes

(a) Both A and R are true and R is the correct explanation of A
(b) Both A and R are true, but R is not the correct explanation of A
(c) A is true, but R is false
(d) A is false, but R is true

23. Identify the personality from the description given below.

- He is popularly known as Parrot of India and Father of Urdu Literature.
- He is credited with the invention of Sitar and Tabla.

(a) Amir Khusrau
(b) Tansen
(c) Hariprasad Chaurasia
(d) Swami Haridas

24. Consider the following statements and choose the correct option.

I. Ustad Zakir Hussain is a professional Tabla player.

II. Pt Ravi Shankar is a professional Sitar player.

III. Pt Hariprasad Chaurasia is a professional Flute player.

Codes

(a) I and II (b) II and III
(c) I and III (d) I, II and III

25.

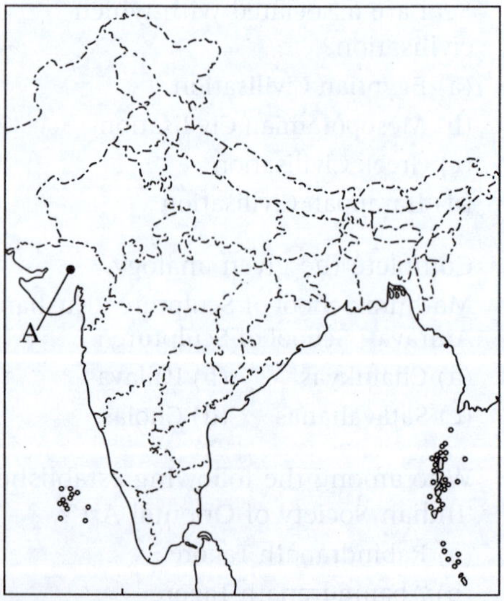

Refer to the marking in the above map and identify the popular dance of the above marked state.

(a) Dandia (b) Bhangra
(c) Garba (d) Both (a) and (c)

Darken your choice with HB Pencil

1.	ⓐ ⓑ ⓒ ⓓ	6.	ⓐ ⓑ ⓒ ⓓ	11.	ⓐ ⓑ ⓒ ⓓ	16.	ⓐ ⓑ ⓒ ⓓ	21.	ⓐ ⓑ ⓒ ⓓ
2.	ⓐ ⓑ ⓒ ⓓ	7.	ⓐ ⓑ ⓒ ⓓ	12.	ⓐ ⓑ ⓒ ⓓ	17.	ⓐ ⓑ ⓒ ⓓ	22.	ⓐ ⓑ ⓒ ⓓ
3.	ⓐ ⓑ ⓒ ⓓ	8.	ⓐ ⓑ ⓒ ⓓ	13.	ⓐ ⓑ ⓒ ⓓ	18.	ⓐ ⓑ ⓒ ⓓ	23.	ⓐ ⓑ ⓒ ⓓ
4.	ⓐ ⓑ ⓒ ⓓ	9.	ⓐ ⓑ ⓒ ⓓ	14.	ⓐ ⓑ ⓒ ⓓ	19.	ⓐ ⓑ ⓒ ⓓ	24.	ⓐ ⓑ ⓒ ⓓ
5.	ⓐ ⓑ ⓒ ⓓ	10.	ⓐ ⓑ ⓒ ⓓ	15.	ⓐ ⓑ ⓒ ⓓ	20.	ⓐ ⓑ ⓒ ⓓ	25.	ⓐ ⓑ ⓒ ⓓ

Chapter 06

Universe

MCQs 1 Mark Questions

1. Who among the following discovered the laws of planetary orbits?
(a) Galileo Galilei
(b) Nicholas Copernicus
(c) Johannes Kepler
(d) Isaac Newton

2. The Earth's axis is tilted at an angle of ....
(a) 23 ½ degrees (b) 66 ½ degrees
(c) 33 ½ degrees (d) 42 ½ degrees

3. What is the outermost layer of the Sun called?
(a) Convection zone
(b) Photosphere
(c) Chromosphere
(d) Corona

4. Find the odd one out from the following options.
(a) Planet (b) Comets
(c) Nebula (d) Moon

5. On which date, the distance between the Earth and the Sun is maximum?
(a) 21st June
(b) 3rd January
(c) 22nd December
(d) 4th July

6. The given below phenomenon is created when a star collapses. Identify it.

(a) Ozone hole (b) Comet
(c) Supernova (d) Planet

7. Which of the following planets does not have any satellites?
(a) Mars and Venus
(b) Mercury and Venus
(c) Mars and Mercury
(d) Neptune and Mars

8. The planet with maximum number of satellites is ....
(a) Uranus (b) Mars
(c) Saturn (d) Neptune

9. The exact time taken by the Earth to rotate on its own axis is ....
(a) 24 hours
(b) 24 hours 35 minutes
(c) 23 hours 50 minutes 7.2 sec
(d) 23 hours 56 minutes 4.09 sec

10. Which planet in the Solar System spins fastest on its axis at the fastest rate?
(a) Neptune (b) Mars
(c) Earth (d) Jupiter

11. Which planet takes maximum time to take one revolution around the Sun?
(a) Saturn (b) Jupiter
(c) Neptune (d) Venus

12. Identify the constellation which is shown in the given picture.

(a) Andromeda
(b) Ursa Minor
(c) Ursa Major
(d) Corona Borealis

13. Complete the given analogy.
Earth : Gravity :: Space : ?
(a) Moon (b) Vacuum
(c) Sun (d) Black hole

14. What would be the colour of the sky if there is no Sun?
(a) Orange (b) Blue
(c) Black (d) Purple

15. Why is Mercury difficult to be seen?
(a) It is too close to the Sun and gets hidden by the glare of the Sun.
(b) It is hidden behind Venus.
(c) It is too far from the Earth.
(d) Because no sunlight falls on it at night.

16. Which among the following is not a jovian planet?
(a) Jupiter (b) Uranus
(c) Saturn (d) Mars

17. Which among the following is not terrestrial planets?
(a) Neptune (b) Mars
(c) Earth (d) Venus

18. How much time does the Sun rays take to reach the Earth?
(a) 10 minutes (b) 8 minutes
(c) 12 minutes (d) 9 minutes

MCQs 2 Marks Questions

19. Match the following.

	List I		List II
A.	Venus	1.	North Star
B.	Black hole	2.	Brightest Star
C.	Pole Star	3.	Morning Star
D.	Sirius	4.	Dead Star

Codes

	A	B	C	D		A	B	C	D
(a)	4	2	1	3	(b)	3	4	2	1
(c)	3	4	1	2	(d)	2	1	4	3

20. Read the following statements and choose the incorrect option.
I. Terrestrial planets are made up of rocks and metals.
II. Mercury is a terrestrial planet.

Codes
(a) Only I (b) Only II
(c) Both I and II (d) None of these

21. Read the following statements and choose the incorrect option.
I. Jovian planets have thin atmospheric layer.
II. Only Mars and Earth are jovian planets.
III. Among all the planets, Earth has the highest density.

Codes
(a) I and II (b) I and III
(c) Only II (d) Only III

22. Read the following statements and identifies which ones are true (T) and which ones are false (F).

I. Asteroid revolves around the Earth.

II. Asteroid belt is located between orbits of Mars and Earth.

III. Meteoroids are small groups of rocks that move around the Sun.

Codes

	I	II	III		I	II	III
(a)	F	F	F	(b)	F	F	T
(c)	T	F	F	(d)	F	T	T

23. There are two statements marked as Assertion (A) and Reason (R). Mark your answer as per the codes given below.

Assertion (A) Moon does not have conditions favourable for life.

Reason (R) There is no water on Moon.

Codes

(a) Both A and R are true and R is the correct explanation of A

(b) Both A and R are true, but R is not the correct explanation of A

(c) A is true, but R is false

(d) A is false, but R is true

24. Identify the solar body with the help of the information given below.

- It is an icy and smaller celestial body which revolves around the Sun in highly elliptical orbit.
- Their period of revolution around the Sun is very long.

(a) Comets

(b) Asteroids

(c) Meteoroids

(d) Planets

25. Read the following statements and identifies which ones are true (T) and which ones are false (F).

I. Moon has constantly cold temperature in its atmosphere.

II. There is an evidence of soil on the surface of the Moon.

III. Full Moon night is known as Amavasya.

Codes

	I	II	III
(a)	T	T	T
(b)	F	F	T
(c)	F	F	F
(d)	T	F	F

Darken your choice with HB Pencil

1.	ⓐ ⓑ ⓒ ⓓ	6.	ⓐ ⓑ ⓒ ⓓ	11.	ⓐ ⓑ ⓒ ⓓ	16.	ⓐ ⓑ ⓒ ⓓ	21.	ⓐ ⓑ ⓒ ⓓ
2.	ⓐ ⓑ ⓒ ⓓ	7.	ⓐ ⓑ ⓒ ⓓ	12.	ⓐ ⓑ ⓒ ⓓ	17.	ⓐ ⓑ ⓒ ⓓ	22.	ⓐ ⓑ ⓒ ⓓ
3.	ⓐ ⓑ ⓒ ⓓ	8.	ⓐ ⓑ ⓒ ⓓ	13.	ⓐ ⓑ ⓒ ⓓ	18.	ⓐ ⓑ ⓒ ⓓ	23.	ⓐ ⓑ ⓒ ⓓ
4.	ⓐ ⓑ ⓒ ⓓ	9.	ⓐ ⓑ ⓒ ⓓ	14.	ⓐ ⓑ ⓒ ⓓ	19.	ⓐ ⓑ ⓒ ⓓ	24.	ⓐ ⓑ ⓒ ⓓ
5.	ⓐ ⓑ ⓒ ⓓ	10.	ⓐ ⓑ ⓒ ⓓ	15.	ⓐ ⓑ ⓒ ⓓ	20.	ⓐ ⓑ ⓒ ⓓ	25.	ⓐ ⓑ ⓒ ⓓ

Chapter 07

Physical Features of India

MCQs 1 Mark Questions

1. Which among the following is the Northernmost range of Himalayas?
   (a) Himadri (b) Himachal
   (c) Shivaliks (d) Trans-Himalayas

2. Identify the mountain peak(s) which is/are located in Himadri range.
   (a) Mt Everest (b) Kanchenjunga
   (c) Nanga Parbat (d) All of these

3. Which of the following hill stations is/are located in lesser Himalayan range?
   (a) Shimla (b) Mussoorie
   (c) Darjeeling (d) All of these

4. Identify the outermost range of Himalayas from the options given below.
   (a) Himachal
   (b) Himadri
   (c) Shivaliks
   (d) Trans-Himalayan range

5. Dehra Dun and Kotli Dun lies in which of the following Himalayan ranges?
   (a) Himachal
   (b) Himadri
   (c) Trans-Himalayas
   (d) Shivaliks

6. Choose the incorrectly matched pair.

Himalayan division	Location
(a) Punjab Himalayas	– Between Indus and Satluj Rivers
(b) Kumaon Himalayas	– Between Indus and Brahmaputra Rivers
(c) Nepal Himalayas	– Between Kali and Teesta Rivers
(d) Assam Himalayas	– Between Teesta and Dihang Rivers

7. Baltoro and Siachen Glaciers are located in .... Himalayas.
   (a) Trans (b) Kashmir
   (c) Kumaon (d) Nepal

8. Complete the given analogy
   Khardung La Pass : Ladakh :: Banihal Pass : ?
   (a) Tibet
   (b) Pir Panjal
   (c) Zanksar
   (d) Shivalik

9. Which among the following is also known as White Mountain?
   (a) Mt Makalu (b) Dhaulagiri
   (c) Nanda Devi (d) Namcha Barwa

10. Which important pilgrimage site(s) is/are located in Himachal Himalayas?
(a) Badrinath (b) Kedarnath
(c) Yamunotri (d) All of these

11. Identify the state(s) that is/are part of the Great Northern Plains of India.
(a) Punjab (b) Haryana
(c) Uttar Pradesh (d) All of these

12. Which region is found along the foothills of Shivaliks from Indus to Teesta?
(a) Bhabhar (b) Terai
(c) Khadar (d) Bhangar

13. Identify region in India which comprises of Ganga-Brahmaputra Delta.
(a) Khadar (b) Terai
(c) Bhangar (d) Bhabhar

14. The Peninsular Plateau is/are spread among which of the following states?
(a) Maharashtra (b) Gujarat
(c) Karnataka (d) All of these

15. Which among the following is/are the part of Central Highlands?
(a) Malwa Plateau
(b) Chota Nagpur Plateau
(c) Deccan Plateau
(d) Both (a) and (b)

16. What is the meaning of the term Deccan Trap?
(a) Land of the Deccan Plateau
(b) Black soil area of the Deccan Plateau
(c) Alluvial soil of Deccan Plateau
(d) Northern region of Narmada region

17. Which among the following is the largest plateau in India?
(a) Chhattisgarh Plateau
(b) Deccan Plateau
(c) Central Highlands
(d) Chota Nagpur Plateau

18. Name the highest peak of South India.
(a) Guru Shikhar
(b) Anaimudi
(c) Mount Abu
(d) Kamet

19. Identify the major river(s) flowing through Western Ghats.
(a) Godavari
(b) Krishna
(c) Tapti
(d) All of the above

20. Which is the highest peak of Eastern Ghats?
(a) Mahendragiri (b) Kathai Betta
(c) Arma Konda (d) Jindhagada Peak

21. Eastern Ghats and Western Ghats meet at which range?
(a) Cardamom Hills
(b) Satpura Range
(c) Nilgiri Hills
(d) Garo Hills

22. Which of the following mountain ranges separates North India from South India?
(a) Satpura Range
(b) Vindhyan Range
(c) Aravalli Range
(d) Rajmahal Hills

23. Identify the oldest mountain range in India.
(a) Western Ghats
(b) Purvanchal Hills
(c) Aravalli
(d) Himadri

24. Choose the only river that flows through the Thar Desert.
(a) Luni
(b) Chenab
(c) Satluj
(d) Jhelum

25. Which activity/activities takes place in the Coastal Plains of India?
(a) Growing of spices, pepper, coconut, etc
(b) Trade and commerce
(c) Fishing
(d) All of the above

26. Identify the largest island of Arabian Sea island group.
(a) Lakshadweep (b) Minicoy
(c) Andaman Island (d) Nicobar Island

MCQs 2 Marks Questions

27. Consider the following statements and choose the correct option.
I. Bhagirathi and Alaknanda together forms Ganga River.
II. Chota Nagpur Plateau is described as the Ruhr of India.
III. Yamuna is the largest tributary of Ganga River.

Codes
(a) I and II (b) II and III
(c) I and III (d) I, II and III

28. Match the following.

List I (Rivers)	**List II** (Tributaries)
A. Indus	1. Jhelum
B. Ganga	2. Kosi
C. Brahmaputra	3. Lohit
D. Yamuna	4. Betwa

Codes
A B C D A B C D
(a) 1 2 3 4 (b) 2 1 4 3
(c) 3 4 2 1 (d) 4 3 1 2

29. Read the following statements and identifies which ones are true (T) and which ones are false (F).
I. Wular Lake and Dal Lake are found in Kashmir Himalayas.
II. Vaishno Devi and Amarnath Caves are located in Darjeeling Himalayas.
III. Namcha Barwa peak lies in Arunachal Himalayas.
IV. Karakoram range lies in North Western Himalayas.

Codes
I II III IV
(a) T T T T
(b) F F F F
(c) T F T T
(d) F T F F

30. Identify the region with the help of the information given below.
- This region is drained by two major river systems viz. Ganga and Indus.
- Hill stations such as Dharamshala, Mussoorie, Kasauli are located in this range.

(a) North-Western Himalayas
(b) Himachal and Uttarakhand Himalayas
(c) Sikkim Himalayas
(d) Eastern Hills

31. There are two statements marked as Assertion (A) and Reason (R). Mark your answer as per the codes given below.
Assertion (A) Peninsular Plateau is a part of Gondwana land.
Reason(R) Narmada River divides Peninsular Plateau into Central Highlands and Deccan Plateau.

Codes

(a) Both A and R are true and R is the correct explanation of A

(b) Both A and R are true, but R is not the correct explanation of A

(c) A is true, but R is false

(d) A is false, but R is true

32. Read the following statements and identifies which ones is/are true (T).

I. Thar Desert is also known as Great Indian Desert.

II. Thar Desert is the ninth largest desert in the world.

Codes

(a) Only I

(b) Only II

(c) Both I and II

(d) None of the above

33. Refer to marked region (A) in the given below map and identify the pass located in the marked region.

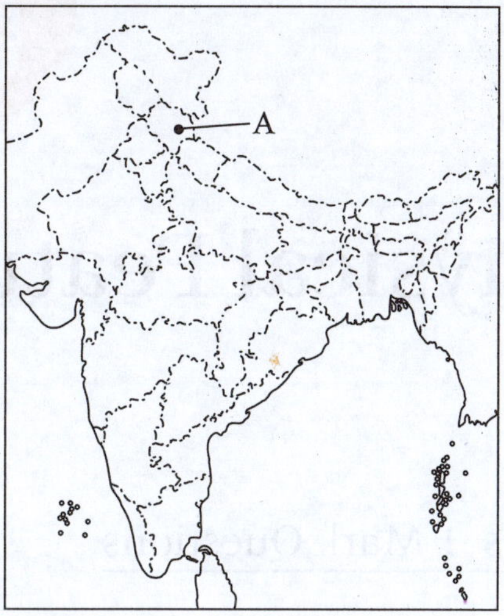

(a) Rohtang Pass (b) Zoji La Pass

(c) Dihang Pass (d) Khardung La Pass

Darken your choice with HB Pencil

1.	ⓐ ⓑ ⓒ ⓓ	7.	ⓐ ⓑ ⓒ ⓓ	13.	ⓐ ⓑ ⓒ ⓓ	19.	ⓐ ⓑ ⓒ ⓓ	25.	ⓐ ⓑ ⓒ ⓓ	31.	ⓐ ⓑ ⓒ ⓓ
2.	ⓐ ⓑ ⓒ ⓓ	8.	ⓐ ⓑ ⓒ ⓓ	14.	ⓐ ⓑ ⓒ ⓓ	20.	ⓐ ⓑ ⓒ ⓓ	26.	ⓐ ⓑ ⓒ ⓓ	32.	ⓐ ⓑ ⓒ ⓓ
3.	ⓐ ⓑ ⓒ ⓓ	9.	ⓐ ⓑ ⓒ ⓓ	15.	ⓐ ⓑ ⓒ ⓓ	21.	ⓐ ⓑ ⓒ ⓓ	27.	ⓐ ⓑ ⓒ ⓓ	33.	ⓐ ⓑ ⓒ ⓓ
4.	ⓐ ⓑ ⓒ ⓓ	10.	ⓐ ⓑ ⓒ ⓓ	16.	ⓐ ⓑ ⓒ ⓓ	22.	ⓐ ⓑ ⓒ ⓓ	28.	ⓐ ⓑ ⓒ ⓓ		
5.	ⓐ ⓑ ⓒ ⓓ	11.	ⓐ ⓑ ⓒ ⓓ	17.	ⓐ ⓑ ⓒ ⓓ	23.	ⓐ ⓑ ⓒ ⓓ	29.	ⓐ ⓑ ⓒ ⓓ		
6.	ⓐ ⓑ ⓒ ⓓ	12.	ⓐ ⓑ ⓒ ⓓ	18.	ⓐ ⓑ ⓒ ⓓ	24.	ⓐ ⓑ ⓒ ⓓ	30.	ⓐ ⓑ ⓒ ⓓ		

Chapter 08

Physical Features of the World

MCQs 1 Mark Questions

1. The African Plateau is famous for which among the following?
(a) Gold
(b) Diamond mining
(c) Iron ores
(d) Both (a) and (b)

2. Where is Mount Kilimanjaro located?
(a) Afghanistan
(b) Libya
(c) Russia
(d) Tanzania

3. Which among the following is/are the major volcanic mountains present in the world?
(a) Mt Kilimanjaro
(b) Mt Fuji
(c) Himalayas
(d) Both (a) and (b)

4. Which among the following is the largest mountain series of the world?
(a) Himalayas (b) Andes
(c) Rockies (d) Alps

5. Highest peaks of the world are found in .... mountains.
(a) young fold
(b) block
(c) old fold
(d) residual

6. Atlas Mountains are situated in which continent?
(a) America
(b) Africa
(c) Europe
(d) Asia

7. Which one of the following is known as the sea of mountains?
(a) Japan
(b) British Columbia
(c) South America
(d) Russia

8. .... Plateau is the highest plateau in the world.
(a) Tibetan
(b) Deccan
(c) Chota Nagpur
(d) African

9. Which among the following plateaus is known as the roof of the world?
(a) Tibetan Plateau
(b) African Plateau
(c) Deccan Plateau
(d) Chota Nagpur Plateau

10. Choose the correctly matched pair(s).
(a) Alps – Europe
(b) Himalaya – Asia
(c) Andes – South America
(d) All of the above

11. Identify the most fertile landforms of the surface of the Earth.
(a) Plateaus
(b) Plains
(c) Hilly regions
(d) Both (a) and (b)

12. The Great Plains is located in which among the following countries?
(a) America (b) China
(c) Russia (d) Germany

13. Which among the following are responsible for the formation of plains?
(a) Lakes
(b) Plateaus
(c) Plains
(d) Rivers and tributaries

14. World's largest numbers of active volcanoes are found in which of the following oceans?
(a) Pacific Ocean
(b) Indian Ocean
(c) Atlantic Ocean
(d) Arctic Ocean

15. Identify the largest cold desert in the world.
(a) Antarctic Desert
(b) Arctic Desert
(c) Kalahari Desert
(d) Gobi Desert

16. Which of the following oceans holds almost 50% of total water on the planet?
(a) Pacific Ocean
(b) Atlantic Ocean
(c) Indian Ocean
(d) Arctic Ocean

17. Bermuda Triangle is located in ....
(a) Indian Ocean
(b) Pacific Ocean
(c) Atlantic Ocean
(d) Arctic Ocean

18. Name the longest river in the world.
(a) Yellow River
(b) Nile River
(c) Amazon River
(d) Indus River

19. Which is the largest river in the world in terms of discharge volume of water?
(a) Nile River
(b) Amazon River
(c) Niger River
(d) Ganga River

20. Name the longest river in Asia.
(a) Yangzte River
(b) Brahmaputra River
(c) Indus River
(d) Ganga River

21. The longest river in Europe is ....
(a) the Rhine
(b) the Volga
(c) the Danube
(d) the Rhone

22. Which among the following is the largest freshwater lake in the world by surface area?
(a) Superior Lake
(b) Michigan Lake
(c) Baikal Lake
(d) Vostok Lake

23. Identify the lake(s) that is/are located in USA.
(a) Michigan Lake
(b) Superior Lake
(c) Ontario Lake
(d) All of the above

24. Identify the sea which is also known as Dead Sea.
(a) Caspian Sea (b) Red Sea
(c) Sargasso Sea (d) Lake Superior

25. Which among the following is the largest hot desert in the world?
(a) Gobi Desert
(b) Atacama Desert
(c) Sahara Desert
(d) Thar Desert

26. The given image is of Gobi Desert. This desert lies in which region?

(a) Asia (b) North America
(c) Europe (d) Australia

27. Name the desert that is located in African region.
(a) Thar Desert
(b) Kalahari Desert
(c) Sahara Desert
(d) Both (b) and (c)

28. Mariana Trench, the deepest ocean trench lies in which ocean?
(a) Atlantic Ocean
(b) Indian Ocean
(c) Pacific Ocean
(d) Arctic Ocean

MCQs 2 Marks Questions

29. Read the following statements and identifies which ones are true (T) and which ones are false (F).

I. Amazon River originates from Andes Mountains.
II. Amazon River is the world's second longest river.
III. Madeira is the largest tributary of the Amazon.
IV. Amazon River drains into Atlantic Ocean.

Codes

	I	II	III	IV
(a)	T	T	T	T
(b)	F	F	F	F
(c)	F	T	F	T
(d)	T	F	T	F

30. Identify the ocean with the help of the description given below.
- It is the third largest ocean in the world.
- It connects three continents namely, Asia, Africa and Australia.

(a) Atlantic Ocean
(b) Pacific Ocean
(c) Indian Ocean
(d) Antarctic Ocean

31. Match the following.

	List I	List II
A.	Thar Desert	1. Africa
B.	Victoria Lake	2. India
C.	Rocky Mountains	3. Russia
D.	Ural Mountains	4. America

Codes

	A	B	C	D
(a)	1	2	3	4
(b)	2	1	4	3
(c)	3	4	2	1
(d)	4	3	1	2

32. There are two statements, marked as Assertion (A) and Reason (R). Mark your answer as per the codes given below.

Assertion (A) The Great Lakes are spread across North America and Canada.

Reason (R) There are ten Great Lakes in America.

Codes

(a) Both A and R are true and R is the correct explanation of A

(b) Both A and R are true, but R is not the correct explanation of A

(c) A is true, but R is false

(d) A is false, but R is true

33. Read the following statements and choose the correct option.

I. The Great Barrier Reef lies in Australia.

II. It is the largest coral reef system of the world.

Codes

(a) Only I (b) Only II

(c) Both I and II (d) None of these

34. Identify the mountains in the marked (A) below region. There is significant biodiversity within the mountain region, with a high number of plants and animal species.

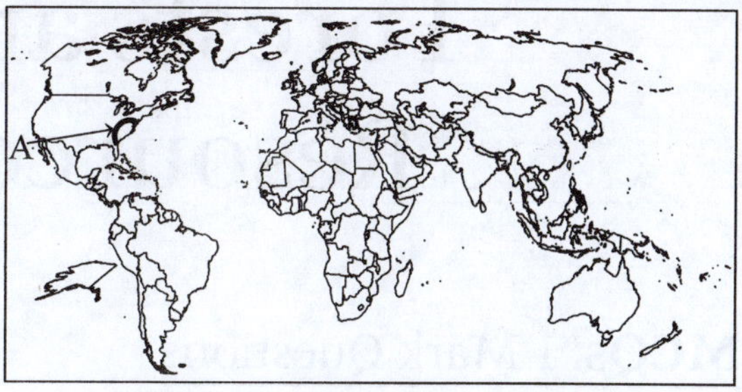

(a) Andes Mountains

(b) Rocky Mountains

(c) Appalachian Mountains

(d) Ural Mountains

Darken your choice with HB Pencil

1.	ⓐ ⓑ ⓒ ⓓ	7.	ⓐ ⓑ ⓒ ⓓ	13.	ⓐ ⓑ ⓒ ⓓ	19.	ⓐ ⓑ ⓒ ⓓ	25.	ⓐ ⓑ ⓒ ⓓ	31.	ⓐ ⓑ ⓒ ⓓ
2.	ⓐ ⓑ ⓒ ⓓ	8.	ⓐ ⓑ ⓒ ⓓ	14.	ⓐ ⓑ ⓒ ⓓ	20.	ⓐ ⓑ ⓒ ⓓ	26.	ⓐ ⓑ ⓒ ⓓ	32.	ⓐ ⓑ ⓒ ⓓ
3.	ⓐ ⓑ ⓒ ⓓ	9.	ⓐ ⓑ ⓒ ⓓ	15.	ⓐ ⓑ ⓒ ⓓ	21.	ⓐ ⓑ ⓒ ⓓ	27.	ⓐ ⓑ ⓒ ⓓ	33.	ⓐ ⓑ ⓒ ⓓ
4.	ⓐ ⓑ ⓒ ⓓ	10.	ⓐ ⓑ ⓒ ⓓ	16.	ⓐ ⓑ ⓒ ⓓ	22.	ⓐ ⓑ ⓒ ⓓ	28.	ⓐ ⓑ ⓒ ⓓ	34.	ⓐ ⓑ ⓒ ⓓ
5.	ⓐ ⓑ ⓒ ⓓ	11.	ⓐ ⓑ ⓒ ⓓ	17.	ⓐ ⓑ ⓒ ⓓ	23.	ⓐ ⓑ ⓒ ⓓ	29.	ⓐ ⓑ ⓒ ⓓ		
6.	ⓐ ⓑ ⓒ ⓓ	12.	ⓐ ⓑ ⓒ ⓓ	18.	ⓐ ⓑ ⓒ ⓓ	24.	ⓐ ⓑ ⓒ ⓓ	30.	ⓐ ⓑ ⓒ ⓓ		

Chapter 09

Forests and Wildlife Resources of India

MCQs 1 Mark Questions

1. Which among the following factors influence the natural vegetation of a place?
(a) Land (b) Rainfall
(c) Temperature (d) All of these

2. Which type of forests occupies the highest percentage of area in India?
(a) Tropical Deciduous
(b) Savanna and Desert Vegetation
(c) Equatorial Evergreen
(d) Tropical Rainforests

3. Identify the incorrectly matched pair.
(a) Tropical Evergreen Forest – Andaman and Nicobar Islands
(b) Tropical Deciduous Forest – Manipur and Mizoram
(c) Thorn Forest – Madhya Pradesh
(d) Temperate Forest – Ladakh

4. Blue sheep, Asiatic elephants and Gangetic dolphins are examples of ....
(a) vulnerable species
(b) rare species
(c) endemic species
(d) extinct species

5. Manas Tiger Reserve is located in ....
(a) Tamil Nadu (b) Kerala
(c) Assam (d) Odisha

6. Which of the following is located in the state of Rajasthan?
(a) Corbett National Park
(b) Bandhavgarh National Park
(c) Periyar Tiger Reserve
(d) Sariska Wildlife Sanctuary

7. Bandipur National Park is located in which of the following states?
(a) Andhra Pradesh (b) Rajasthan
(c) Assam (d) Karnataka

8. .... forests in India are home to White Tiger.
(a) Sundarbans
(b) Gir Forest
(c) Bandhavgarh Forest
(d) Namdapha Forest

9. Complete the given analogy.
Jim Corbett National Park : Uttarakhand : : Kudremukh National Park : ?
(a) Karnataka (b) Kerala
(c) Tamil Nadu (d) Assam

10. Which of the following species of trees are found in the forest of Himalayan region?
(a) Pines (b) Cedars
(c) Fir (d) All of these

11. Sundarbans in India are an example of which type of forest?
(a) Moist Deciduous Forest
(b) Dry Deciduous Forest
(c) Littoral and Swamp Forest
(d) Evergreen Forest

12. Choose the state that has highest number of national parks in India.
(a) Uttarakhand (b) Maharashtra
(c) Madhya Pradesh (d) Assam

13. Which types of forests are usually managed by local communities?
(a) Reserved Forests
(b) Protected Forests
(c) Unclassed Forests
(d) Wildlife Sanctuaries

14. Choose an important species that is found in Wet Evergreen Forests.
(a) Bamboo (b) Cedar
(c) Rosewood (d) Mango

15. Kaziranga National Park that was declared as UNESCO World Heritage Site is famous for which among the following?
(a) Royal Bengal Tiger
(b) One-horned Rhinoceros
(c) Jackals
(d) Asiatic Cheetah

16. Royal Bengal Tiger is the famous animal of which of the following forests?
(a) Montane Forests
(b) Tropical Deciduous Forests
(c) Tropical Thorn Forests and Scrubs
(d) Mangrove Forests

17. Hemis National Park is located in which State/UT?
(a) Jammu and Kashmir
(b) Uttarakhand
(c) Puducherry
(d) Bihar

18. Which type of forests are found in Gujarat and Rajasthan?
(a) Montane Forests
(b) Thorn Forests and Scrubs
(c) Tropical Evergreen Forests
(d) Montane Forests

MCQs 2 Marks Questions

19. Match the following.

	List I		List II
A.	Bandhavgarh National Park	1.	Maharashtra
B.	Tadoba National Park	2.	Madhya Pradesh
C.	Similipal National Park	3.	Uttar Pradesh
D.	Dudhwa National Park	4.	Odisha

Codes

	A	B	C	D		A	B	C	D
(a)	1	2	3	4	(b)	2	1	4	3
(c)	3	4	2	1	(d)	4	3	1	2

20. Identify the national park with the help of the information given below.
- It is the first national park established in India.
- The park was the first to come under the Project Tiger initiative.

(a) Kaziranga National Park
(b) Jim Corbett National Park
(c) Similipal National Park
(d) Kanha National Park

21. Consider the following statements and choose the correct option.

I. Tiger is an endangered species.

II. Project Tiger was launched in 1973.

III. Sundarbans National Park and Bandhavgarh National Park are some important Tiger Reserves in India.

Codes

(a) I and II (b) II and III

(c) I and III (d) I, II and III

22. Read the following statements and identifies which ones are true (T) and which ones are false (F).

I. Valley of Flowers National Park is located in Uttarakhand.

II. Buxa Tiger Reserve is located in West Bengal.

III. Gir National Park is the only habitat of Asiatic Lion in the world.

Codes

	I	II	III		I	II	III
(a)	T	T	T	(b)	F	F	F
(c)	F	T	F	(d)	T	F	T

23. Read the following statements and choose the correct option.

I. Tropical Wet Evergreen Forests are found in the region where rainfall exceeds 250 cm.

II. In Evergreen Forests, trees do not shed their leaves altogether and hence remain evergreen.

Codes

(a) Only I

(b) Only II

(c) Both I and II

(d) None of the above

24. Identify the national park located in the given marked state (A), which is a UNESCO Natural World Heritage Site.

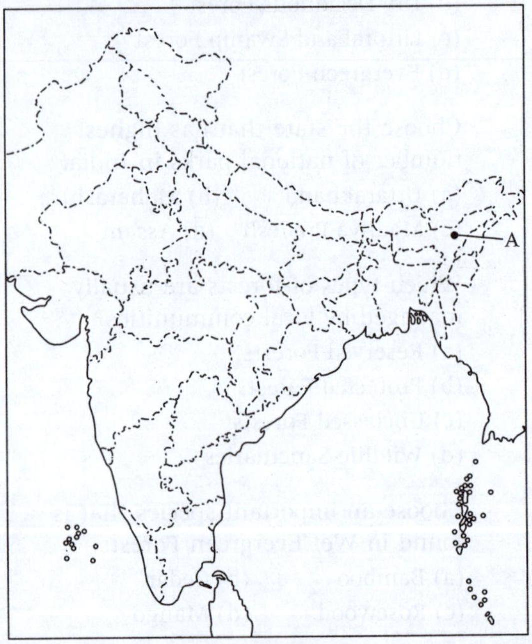

(a) Manas National Park

(b) Eravikulam National Park

(c) Valmiki National Park

(d) Indravati National Park

Darken your choice with HB Pencil

1.	ⓐ ⓑ ⓒ ⓓ	5.	ⓐ ⓑ ⓒ ⓓ	9.	ⓐ ⓑ ⓒ ⓓ	13.	ⓐ ⓑ ⓒ ⓓ	17.	ⓐ ⓑ ⓒ ⓓ	21.	ⓐ ⓑ ⓒ ⓓ
2.	ⓐ ⓑ ⓒ ⓓ	6.	ⓐ ⓑ ⓒ ⓓ	10.	ⓐ ⓑ ⓒ ⓓ	14.	ⓐ ⓑ ⓒ ⓓ	18.	ⓐ ⓑ ⓒ ⓓ	22.	ⓐ ⓑ ⓒ ⓓ
3.	ⓐ ⓑ ⓒ ⓓ	7.	ⓐ ⓑ ⓒ ⓓ	11.	ⓐ ⓑ ⓒ ⓓ	15.	ⓐ ⓑ ⓒ ⓓ	19.	ⓐ ⓑ ⓒ ⓓ	23.	ⓐ ⓑ ⓒ ⓓ
4.	ⓐ ⓑ ⓒ ⓓ	8.	ⓐ ⓑ ⓒ ⓓ	12.	ⓐ ⓑ ⓒ ⓓ	16.	ⓐ ⓑ ⓒ ⓓ	20.	ⓐ ⓑ ⓒ ⓓ	24.	ⓐ ⓑ ⓒ ⓓ

Chapter 10

Weather and Climate

MCQs 1 Mark Questions

1. Which part of India receives rainfall from both the South-West and North-West monsoons?
(a) Tamil Nadu
(b) Odisha
(c) Lakshadweep Islands
(d) Andaman and Nicobar Islands

2. Identify the region which receives the first monsoon in summer.
(a) Himalayas
(b) Western Ghats
(c) Eastern Ghats
(d) Gangetic Plain

3. The pre-monsoon mango showers occur predominantly in .... and ....
(a) West Bengal and Assam
(b) Maharashtra and Kerala
(c) Gujarat and Maharashtra
(d) Kerala and Karnataka

4. Which of the following states receives rainfall due to Western disturbances?
(a) Punjab (b) West Bengal
(c) Kerala (d) Gujarat

5. The Western Coast gets heaviest rainfall during ..... due to South-West monsoons.
(a) June
(b) August
(c) October
(d) January

6. The Eastern Coast gets maximum rainfall during which season?
(a) Summer season
(b) Rainy season
(c) Winter season
(d) Spring season

7. Which among the following is said to bring rains in India?
(a) El Nino
(b) La Nina
(c) ITCZ
(d) Both (a) and (b)

8. Identify the phenomenon that causes widespread floods and droughts in the tropicals of the world including India.
(a) El Nino
(b) La Nina
(b) Westerlies
(d) Loo

9. Choose the driest place in India from the given below options.
(a) Leh
(b) Jaisalmer
(c) Cherrapunji
(d) Kashmir

10. Which place in India receives lowest rainfall?
(a) Leh
(b) Kashmir
(c) Jaisalmer
(d) Bhuj

11. Name the place which experiences extreme type of climate.
(a) Mumbai
(b) Delhi
(c) Pune
(d) Bengaluru

12. In which of the following regions, we can find polar type of climate in India?
(a) Ladakh
(b) Delhi
(c) Kolkata
(d) Punjab

13. Monsoon winds comprises of which types of winds?
(a) Seasonal winds
(b) Trade winds
(c) Loo
(d) Local winds

14. Which one of the following states receives the highest rainfall during winter months?
(a) Punjab
(b) Kerala
(c) Meghalaya
(d) Tamil Nadu

15. Choose the characteristics of cold weather season in India.
(a) Warm days and warm nights
(b) Warm days and cold nights
(c) Cold days and cold nights
(d) Cold days and warm nights

16. Wind blowing in Northern plains during summers is known by ....
(a) Loo (b) Trade winds
(c) Westerlies (d) Seasonal winds

MCQs 2 Marks Questions

17. Consider the following statements and choose the correct option.
I. Himalayan mountains do not affect the climate of India.
II. India experiences tropical monsoon type of climate.

Codes
(a) Only I
(b) Only II
(c) Both I and II
(d) None of the above

18. Read the following statements and identifies which ones are true (T) and which ones are false (F).
I. Temperature increases with increase in height.
II. Places in mountains are cooler than places on plains.
III. Indian climate is also characterised by natural calamities such as droughts and floods.

Codes

	I	II	III
(a)	T	T	T
(b)	F	F	F
(c)	F	T	F
(d)	F	T	T

19. Read the following statements and choose the correct option.

I. Indian monsoon is seasonal in character.

II. Monsoon rainfall declines with increase in the distance from the sea.

Codes

(a) Only I

(b) Only II

(c) Both I and II

(d) None of the above

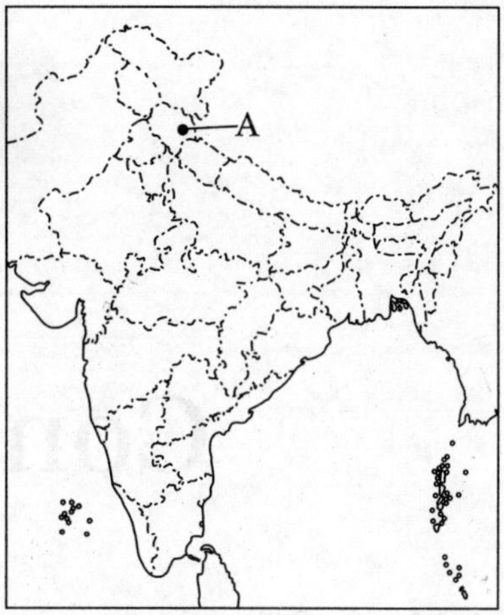

20. Refer to the state marked (A) in the given map. Which type of climate is experienced by the marked state?

(a) Polar climate

(b) Monsoon climate

(c) Hot desert climate

(d) Tropical Savanna climate

Darken your choice with HB Pencil

1.	ⓐ	ⓑ	ⓒ	ⓓ	5.	ⓐ	ⓑ	ⓒ	ⓓ	9.	ⓐ	ⓑ	ⓒ	ⓓ	13.	ⓐ	ⓑ	ⓒ	ⓓ	17.	ⓐ	ⓑ	ⓒ	ⓓ
2.	ⓐ	ⓑ	ⓒ	ⓓ	6.	ⓐ	ⓑ	ⓒ	ⓓ	10.	ⓐ	ⓑ	ⓒ	ⓓ	14.	ⓐ	ⓑ	ⓒ	ⓓ	18.	ⓐ	ⓑ	ⓒ	ⓓ
3.	ⓐ	ⓑ	ⓒ	ⓓ	7.	ⓐ	ⓑ	ⓒ	ⓓ	11.	ⓐ	ⓑ	ⓒ	ⓓ	15.	ⓐ	ⓑ	ⓒ	ⓓ	19.	ⓐ	ⓑ	ⓒ	ⓓ
4.	ⓐ	ⓑ	ⓒ	ⓓ	8.	ⓐ	ⓑ	ⓒ	ⓓ	12.	ⓐ	ⓑ	ⓒ	ⓓ	16.	ⓐ	ⓑ	ⓒ	ⓓ	20.	ⓐ	ⓑ	ⓒ	ⓓ

Chapter 11

Continents

MCQs 1 Mark Questions

1. Which of the following is the second largest continent in the world?
(a) Asia (b) Africa
(c) Antarctica (d) Australia

2. The continent Asia shares its Eastern border with ....
(a) Africa (b) Arctic Ocean
(c) Pacific Ocean (d) Ural Mountains

3. The highest mountain of the world Mount Everest is located in which continent?
(a) Asia (b) Antarctica
(c) Australia (d) North America

4. Which is the lowest point of the Asian continent?
(a) Mount Everest
(b) Dead Sea
(c) Deccan Plateau
(d) Ural Mountains

5. Identify the island(s) which is/are located in Asian continent.
(a) Java (b) Philippines
(c) Sri Lanka (d) All of these

6. Out of seven continents, the continent Europe shares its West boundary with which of the following?
(a) Arctic Ocean
(b) Atlantic Ocean
(c) Mediterranean Sea
(d) Ural Mountains

7. Which peninsula(s) is/are located in Asian Continent?
(a) Malay Peninsula
(b) Indian Peninsula
(c) Arabian Peninsula
(d) All of the above

8. Asia shares its North border with ....
(a) Africa (b) Arctic Ocean
(c) Pacific Ocean (d) Ural Mountains

9. Which is the largest country in South American continent?
(a) Peru (b) Argentina
(c) Brazil (d) Venezuela

10. The continent Europe shares its South boundary with which among the following?
(a) Arctic Ocean (b) Atlantic Ocean
(c) Mediterranean Sea (d) Ural Mountains

11. Which of the following seas separates Africa from Asia?
(a) Baltic Sea
(b) Black Sea
(c) Mediterranean Sea
(d) Red Sea

12. Identify the continent which lies within Western and Northern Hemisphere of the globe.
(a) Africa (b) North America
(c) South America (d) Asia

13. Which of the following countries does not lie within African continent?
(a) Libya (b) France
(c) Sudan (d) Congo

14. Asia shares its South border with ....
(a) Indian Ocean (b) Mediterranean Sea
(c) Pacific Ocean (d) Atlantic Ocean

15. The world's coldest Antarctica continent is surrounded by ....
(a) Western Ocean (b) Southern Ocean
(c) Northern Ocean (d) Eastern Ocean

16. Which continent is situated between the Atlantic and Pacific Ocean?
(a) Africa (b) Asia
(c) South America (d) North America

17. Identify the incorrectly matched pair.
(a) Asia – China
(b) South America – Canada
(c) Africa – Sudan
(d) Australia – New Zealand

18. Complete the given analogy.
Africa : Nigeria : : Asia : ?
(a) Brazil (b) Venezuela
(c) Thailand (d) Greece

19. Identify the country which does not lie within North America continent.
(a) Panama (b) Mexico
(c) Ethiopia (d) Cuba

20. Which sea separates the Africa continent from the Europe continent?
(a) Baltic Sea
(b) Black Sea
(c) Mediterranean Sea
(d) Red Sea

21. Name the largest continent in terms of area and population.
(a) Africa (b) Asia
(c) Europe (d) Australia

22. Which among the following is the largest lake of the world that lies in Asia?
(a) Caspian Sea (b) Lake Superior
(c) Lake Victoria (d) Lake Bled

23. The given picture depicts the only continent through which Tropic of Cancer, Tropic of Capricorn and Equator passes. Identify the continent.

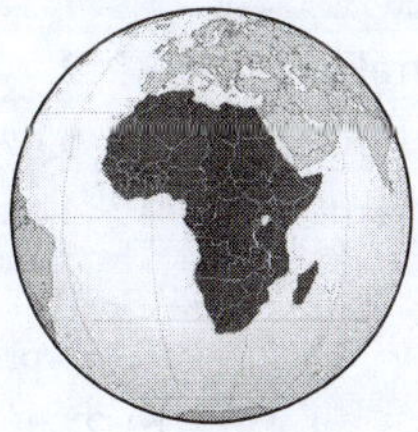

(a) Asia (b) Africa
(c) Europe (d) Australia

24. Identify the island(s) that lies in the North American continent.
(a) Greenland (b) Cuba
(c) Hawaii (d) All of these

25. Which country in the North American continent has longest coastline?
(a) Canada (b) Mexico
(c) Cuba (d) Costa Rica

26. Lake Superior is the largest sweet water lake in the world. It lies in which continent?
(a) North America (b) South America
(c) Europe (d) Australia

27. Which continent is also known as Forgotten Land?

(a) Europe (b) South America
(c) Australia (d) Antarctica

MCQs 2 Marks Questions

28. Consider the following statements and choose the correct option.

I. Antarctica is known as White Continent.

II. Great Barrier Reef, largest coral reef in the world lies in Australia.

III. Australia lies between Pacific and Indian Ocean.

Codes

(a) I and II (b) II and III
(c) I and III (d) I, II and III

29. Match the following.

	List I (Continent)		List II (Desert)
A.	Africa	1.	Sahara Desert
B.	Australia	2.	Great Victoria
C.	South America	3.	Atacama
D.	Asia	4.	Gobi

Codes

	A	B	C	D		A	B	C	D
(a)	1	2	3	4	(b)	2	1	4	3
(c)	3	4	2	1	(d)	4	3	1	2

30. Identify the continent from the description given below.

- It is also known as dark continent.
- Kalahari Desert is located in this continent.
- Lake Victoria is one of the largest falls in the world lies in this continent.

(a) Australia (b) Asia
(c) Africa (d) Europe

31. Read the following statements and identifies which ones are true (T) and which ones are false (F).

I. Pakistan in the Asian continent is known as land of canals.

II. Myanmar in the Asian continent is known as land of mountains and rivers.

III. Amazon River lies in the North American continent.

IV. North America is the smallest continent in the world.

Codes

	I	II	III	IV		I	II	III	IV
(a)	T	T	T	T	(b)	F	F	F	F
(c)	F	T	F	T	(d)	T	T	F	F

32. Identify the continent which is shown in the map given below. It is a continent comprising the Westernmost Peninsulas of Eurasia.

(a) South America (b) Australia
(c) Europe (d) Asia

Darken your choice with HB Pencil

1.	ⓐ ⓑ ⓒ ⓓ	7.	ⓐ ⓑ ⓒ ⓓ	13.	ⓐ ⓑ ⓒ ⓓ	19.	ⓐ ⓑ ⓒ ⓓ	25.	ⓐ ⓑ ⓒ ⓓ	31.	ⓐ ⓑ ⓒ ⓓ
2.	ⓐ ⓑ ⓒ ⓓ	8.	ⓐ ⓑ ⓒ ⓓ	14.	ⓐ ⓑ ⓒ ⓓ	20.	ⓐ ⓑ ⓒ ⓓ	26.	ⓐ ⓑ ⓒ ⓓ	32.	ⓐ ⓑ ⓒ ⓓ
3.	ⓐ ⓑ ⓒ ⓓ	9.	ⓐ ⓑ ⓒ ⓓ	15.	ⓐ ⓑ ⓒ ⓓ	21.	ⓐ ⓑ ⓒ ⓓ	27.	ⓐ ⓑ ⓒ ⓓ		
4.	ⓐ ⓑ ⓒ ⓓ	10.	ⓐ ⓑ ⓒ ⓓ	16.	ⓐ ⓑ ⓒ ⓓ	22.	ⓐ ⓑ ⓒ ⓓ	28.	ⓐ ⓑ ⓒ ⓓ		
5.	ⓐ ⓑ ⓒ ⓓ	11.	ⓐ ⓑ ⓒ ⓓ	17.	ⓐ ⓑ ⓒ ⓓ	23.	ⓐ ⓑ ⓒ ⓓ	29.	ⓐ ⓑ ⓒ ⓓ		
6.	ⓐ ⓑ ⓒ ⓓ	12.	ⓐ ⓑ ⓒ ⓓ	18.	ⓐ ⓑ ⓒ ⓓ	24.	ⓐ ⓑ ⓒ ⓓ	30.	ⓐ ⓑ ⓒ ⓓ		

Chapter 12

Ecology and Environment

MCQs 1 Mark Questions

1. Identify the person who is credited for introducing the term biodiversity.
(a) Walter Rosen
(b) Charles Darwin
(c) Ronald Fisher
(d) William Harvey

2. Which among the following is an example of natural ecosystem?
(a) Zoo
(b) Agricultural crop fields
(c) Botanical parks
(d) Teak forests

3. .... is also known as the world of living organisms.
(a) Natural environment
(b) Biotic environment
(c) Cultural environment
(d) Man-made environment

4. Which among the following elements is/are provided by lithosphere?
(a) Forests (b) Grasslands
(c) Land (d) All of these

5. Which among the following is/are the major part of hydrosphere?
(a) Oceans (b) Rivers
(c) Lakes (d) All of these

6. .... is a narrow zone where land, water and air are linked together.
(a) Biosphere (b) Lithosphere
(c) Hydrosphere (d) Atmosphere

7. Identify the incorrectly matched pair.
(a) Abiotic environment – Rainfall
(b) Biotic environment – Human beings
(c) Man-made environment – Land
(d) Cultural environment – Religion

8. Which among the following is/are the part of natural environment?
(a) Hydrosphere (b) Atmosphere
(c) Lithosphere (d) All of these

9. Choose the abiotic component of environment from the given below options.
(a) Plants (b) Decomposers
(c) Sunlight (d) Animals

10. Who used the term ecology for the first time?
(a) Ernst Haeckel
(b) Charles Darwin
(c) Johannes Kepler
(d) Albert Einstein

11. Identify the ecological factor(s) that influence the living organisms.
(a) Temperature (b) Light
(c) Rainfall (d) All of these

12. Which among the following is not a part of biotic component of ecosystem?
(a) Producers
(b) Consumers
(c) Decomposers
(d) Organic components

13. What is/are the parts of decomposers?
(a) Vultures (b) Crow
(c) Bacteria (d) All of these

14. Which is not a part of a terrestrial ecosystem?
(a) Grassland ecosystem
(b) Forest ecosystem
(c) Lake ecosystem
(d) Desert ecosystem

15. Which of the following factors is not involved in the process of Water Cycle?
(a) Precipitation (b) Transportation
(c) transpiration (d) Evaporation

16. Which among the following is not the factor that affect the ecosystem?
(a) Temperature (b) Earthquake
(c) Water (d) Sunlight

17. Identify the example of autotrophs.
(a) Eagle (b) Lion
(c) Algae (d) Humans

18. Identify the organic molecules which is made up of nitrogen.
(a) DNA (b) RNA
(c) Lipids (d) Both (a) and (b)

19. Which among the following is an example of heterotrophs?
(a) Bacteria (b) Plants
(c) Green Algae (d) Fish

20. Which process fixes carbon dioxide from the atmosphere?
(a) Photosynthesis (b) Diffusion
(c) Respiration (d) Condensation

21. Which among the following is on the top of the ecological pyramid?
(a) Decomposers
(b) Primary Consumers
(c) Heterotrophs
(d) Tertiary Consumers

22. Name the international treaty that aims to protect ozone layer from depletion.
(a) Montreal Protocol
(b) Paris Agreement
(c) Ramsar Convention
(d) Kyoto Protocol

23. Which among the following may decrease the harmful effects of Greenhouse Effect on the Earth?
(a) Inter cropping
(b) Afforestation
(c) Evapotranspiration
(d) Respiration

MCQs 2 Marks Questions

24. Which of the following are the components of an ecosystem?
I. Microorganisms
II. Human beings
III. Animals
IV. Soil
Codes
(a) I, II and III (b) I, II and IV
(c) II, III and IV (d) All of these

25. What is/are the consequences of global warming and climate change?
I. Rise in sea level
II. Increse in global temperature
III. Rise in number of wetlands
Codes
(a) I, II, III (b) I and III
(c) II and III (d) I and II

26. Match the following.

	List I (Organism)	**List II** (Type)
A.	Primary Consumers	1. Plant eating animals
B.	Decomposers	2. Bacteria
C.	Scavengers	3. Vultures

Codes

	A	B	C		A	B	C
(a)	3	1	2	(b)	2	1	3
(c)	1	3	2	(d)	1	2	3

27. Consider the following statements and choose the correct option.

I. The herbivores occupy the second trophic level in a food chain.

II. The nutrients from dead animals are recycled by decomposers in a food chain.

III. In a grazing food chain, first level starts with plants.

Codes

(a) Only I (b) Only II

(c) Only III (d) All of these

28. Which among the following steps can certainly help in reducing ozone depletion?

I. Reducing the use of air conditioners

II. Using electric bikes and cars

III. Reducing forest and tree cover

Codes

(a) Both I and III

(b) I, II and III

(c) Both I and II

(d) Both II and III

29. Read the following statements and identify which ones are true (T) and which ones are false (F).

I. Green plants are not the part of producers in an ecosystem.

II. Snakes, tigers are the part of carnivores in an ecosystem.

III. Decomposers do not feed on dead at every level in an ecosystem.

Codes

	I	II	III		I	II	III
(a)	T	T	T	(b)	F	T	T
(c)	F	T	F	(d)	T	F	F

Darken your choice with HB Pencil

1.	ⓐ ⓑ ⓒ ⓓ	6.	ⓐ ⓑ ⓒ ⓓ	11.	ⓐ ⓑ ⓒ ⓓ	16.	ⓐ ⓑ ⓒ ⓓ	21.	ⓐ ⓑ ⓒ ⓓ	26.	ⓐ ⓑ ⓒ ⓓ
2.	ⓐ ⓑ ⓒ ⓓ	7.	ⓐ ⓑ ⓒ ⓓ	12.	ⓐ ⓑ ⓒ ⓓ	17.	ⓐ ⓑ ⓒ ⓓ	22.	ⓐ ⓑ ⓒ ⓓ	27.	ⓐ ⓑ ⓒ ⓓ
3.	ⓐ ⓑ ⓒ ⓓ	8.	ⓐ ⓑ ⓒ ⓓ	13.	ⓐ ⓑ ⓒ ⓓ	18.	ⓐ ⓑ ⓒ ⓓ	23.	ⓐ ⓑ ⓒ ⓓ	28.	ⓐ ⓑ ⓒ ⓓ
4.	ⓐ ⓑ ⓒ ⓓ	9.	ⓐ ⓑ ⓒ ⓓ	14.	ⓐ ⓑ ⓒ ⓓ	19.	ⓐ ⓑ ⓒ ⓓ	24.	ⓐ ⓑ ⓒ ⓓ	29.	ⓐ ⓑ ⓒ ⓓ
5.	ⓐ ⓑ ⓒ ⓓ	10.	ⓐ ⓑ ⓒ ⓓ	15.	ⓐ ⓑ ⓒ ⓓ	20.	ⓐ ⓑ ⓒ ⓓ	25.	ⓐ ⓑ ⓒ ⓓ		

Chapter 13

Sectors of Indian Economy

MCQs 1 Mark Questions

1. Which of the following is also known as disguised employment?
   (a) Over employment
   (b) Factory employment
   (c) Under employment
   (d) Unemployment

2. When did the NREGA (National Rural Employment Guarantee Act) launched in India ?
   (a) 2000
   (b) 2005
   (c) 2010
   (d) 2001

3. Which sector has emerged as the largest producing sector in India?
   (a) Secondary sector
   (b) Tertiary sector
   (c) Primary sector
   (d) Science and Technology sector

4. Which among the following occupations cannot be categorised under tertiary sector?
   (a) Software
   (b) Hospitals
   (c) ATM centres
   (d) Steel manufacturing

5. Which of the following examples does not fall under unorganised sector?
   (a) A farmer irrigating his field.
   (b) A daily wage labourer working for a contractor.
   (c) A doctor in a hospital treating a patient.
   (d) A handloom weaver working on a loom in her house.

6. Which among the following is/are the way(s) to generate more employment in agricultural sector?
   (a) Providing bank credit
   (b) Construction of dams and canals
   (c) Focus on small scale industries
   (d) All of the above

7. Which among the following is not a public sector industry?
   (a) Indian Railways
   (b) Bharat Heavy Electrical Limited
   (c) Hindustan Aeronautics Limited
   (d) Tata and Sons

8. Identify the example(s) of private sector industry from the options given below.
   (a) Reliance Industries
   (b) Birla Industries
   (c) Volkswagen
   (d) All of the above

9. Which of the following roles is not played by public sector industries?
(a) Developing infrastructure
(b) Supporting farmers
(c) Making profits
(d) Provision of healthcare and education

10. The secondary sector is also called as ....
(a) organised sector (b) service sector
(c) industrial sector (d) public sector

11. Identify the sector that acts as aid and support to other sectors.
(a) Primary sector (b) Secondary sector
(c) Tertiary sector (d) Unorganised sector

12. The given picture is of jaggery making. This activity comes under which sector?

(a) Primary sector
(b) Secondary sector
(c) Tertiary sector
(d) Non-economic sector

13. On which of the following basis, the sectors are classified into public and private sector?
(a) Employment conditions
(b) The nature of economic activity
(c) Ownership of enterprises
(d) Number of workers employed in an enterprises

14. 

The above activity is a part of which sector?
(a) Secondary sector
(b) Unorganised sector
(c) Primary sector
(d) Tertiary sector

15. Identify the sector which emerged as the largest producing sector in India.
(a) Primary sector
(b) Tertiary sector
(c) Secondary sector
(d) Science and Technology sector

MCQs 2 Marks Questions

16. There are two statements marked as Assertion (A) and Reason (R). Mark your answer as per the codes given below.
Assertion (A) Primary sector is directly associated with nature.
Reason (R) Primary sector of economy involves conversion of natural resources into primary products.
Codes
(a) Both A and R are true and R is the correct explanation of A
(b) Both A and R are true, but R is not the correct explanation of A
(c) A is true, but R is false
(d) A is false, but R is true

17. Read the following statements and choose the correct option.

I. Bengaluru is an important hub of Information and Technology sector in India.

II. It is also known as the Silicon Valley of India.

Codes

(a) Only I

(b) Only II

(c) Both I and II

(d) Neither I nor II

18. Identify the correct option regarding the various sectors in the descending order based on their contribution to India's GDP

I. Primary Sector

II. Secondary Sector

III. Tertiary Sector

Codes

(a) I, III, II

(b) I, II, III

(c) II, III, I

(d) III, II, I

19. Identify the sector of Indian economy with the help of information given below.

- It is associated with different kinds of industries. Thus, it is also called industrial sector.
- It includes the industries where finished products are made from natural materials produced in the primary sector.

Codes

(a) Organised sector

(b) Quaternery sector

(c) Secondary sector

(d) Primary sector

Darken your choice with HB Pencil

1.	ⓐ ⓑ ⓒ ⓓ	5.	ⓐ ⓑ ⓒ ⓓ	9.	ⓐ ⓑ ⓒ ⓓ	13.	ⓐ ⓑ ⓒ ⓓ	17.	ⓐ ⓑ ⓒ ⓓ
2.	ⓐ ⓑ ⓒ ⓓ	6.	ⓐ ⓑ ⓒ ⓓ	10.	ⓐ ⓑ ⓒ ⓓ	14.	ⓐ ⓑ ⓒ ⓓ	18.	ⓐ ⓑ ⓒ ⓓ
3.	ⓐ ⓑ ⓒ ⓓ	7.	ⓐ ⓑ ⓒ ⓓ	11.	ⓐ ⓑ ⓒ ⓓ	15.	ⓐ ⓑ ⓒ ⓓ	19.	ⓐ ⓑ ⓒ ⓓ
4.	ⓐ ⓑ ⓒ ⓓ	8.	ⓐ ⓑ ⓒ ⓓ	12.	ⓐ ⓑ ⓒ ⓓ	16.	ⓐ ⓑ ⓒ ⓓ		

Chapter 14

Agriculture

MCQs 1 Mark Questions

1. Which of the following are plantation crops?
(a) Rice and maize
(b) Wheat and pulses
(c) Tea, banana and sugarcane
(d) None of the above

2. What are the three major cropping seasons of India?
(a) Aus, aman, boro
(b) Rabi, kharif, zaid
(c) Baisakhi, paus, chait
(d) None of the above

3. The main food crop of kharif season is ....
(a) mustard (b) pulses
(c) rice (d) wheat

4. Identify the main food crop of rabi season.
(a) Wheat (b) Rice
(c) Maize (d) Jowar

5. A short season between the rabi and kharif season is known as ....
(a) aus
(b) boro
(c) zaid
(d) None of the above

6. What is the main food crop of the Eastern and Southern part of India?
(a) Rice (b) Wheat
(c) Maize (d) Sugarcane

7. Which among the following states is the largest producer of bajra?
(a) Rajasthan (b) Bihar
(c) Assam (d) Odisha

8. Which of the following crops is a major source of protein in a vegetarian diet?
(a) Wheat (b) Rice
(c) Pulses (d) Oilseeds

9. Coffee cultivation was first introduced in ....
(a) Shivalik Hills
(b) Aravalli Hills
(c) Garo Hills
(d) Baba Budan Hills

10. Which of the following crops is an important raw material for automobile industry?
(a) Pulses (b) Jute
(c) Rubber (d) None of these

11. Rearing of silkworms for the production of silk fibre is known as ....
(a) sericulture (b) aquaculture
(c) apiculture (d) pisciculture

12. Which one of the following describes a system of agriculture where a single crop is grown on a large area?
(a) Shifting agriculture
(b) Plantation agriculture
(c) Horticulture
(d) Intensive agriculture

13. Which one of the following is announced by the government in support of a crop?
(a) Maximum Support Price
(b) Minimum Support Price
(c) Moderate Support Price
(d) Influential Support Price

14. Cultivation of coffee is confined to which of the following hills?
(a) Nilgiri (b) Aravalli
(c) Shivalik (d) None of these

15. Identify the country which is the largest producer of fruits and vegetables in the world.
(a) China (b) USA
(c) Pakistan (d) India

16. Which one of the following is not a fibre crop?
(a) Cotton (b) Rubber (c) Jute (d) Hemp

17. Plantation agriculture is a type of ....
(a) subsistence farming
(b) commercial farming
(c) mixed farming
(d) None of the above

18. Where was coffee production introduced in India?
(a) Annamala hills (b) Baba burdan hills
(c) Cardamom hills (d) Palani hills

19. The .... agriculture is known as Milpa in Mexico.
(a) extensive (b) intensive
(c) plantation (d) slash and burn

20. Identify the main food crop of the Eastern and Southern part of the country.
(a) Maize (b) Wheat
(c) Sugarcane (d) Rice

21. Which among the following is the largest producer of sugarcane in India?
(a) Tamil Nadu
(b) Uttar Pradesh
(c) Punjab
(d) Odisha

MCQs 2 Marks Questions

22. Read the following statements and identifies which ones are true (T) and which ones are false (F).
I. Shifting agriculture is also known as slash and burn agriculture.
II. Primitive subsistence farming is practiced on small patched of land with basic tools.
III. Intensive subsistence farming is practiced in the areas of high population.

Codes

	I	II	III		I	II	III
(a)	T	T	F	(b)	F	F	F
(c)	T	F	T	(d)	T	T	T

23. There are two statements marked as Assertion (A) and Reason (R). Mark your answer as per the codes given below.
Assertion (A) Fodder crops are grown during zaid season.
Reason (R) Zaid season occurs between kharif and rabi season.

Codes
(a) Both A and R are true and R is the correct explanation of A
(b) Both A and R are true, but R is not the correct explanation of A
(c) A is true, but R is false
(d) A is false, but R is true

24. Match the following.

List I (Types of Vegetation)	List II (Crops)
A. Food crops	1. Oilseeds
B. Cash crops	2. Rubber
C. Horticulture crops	3. Vegetables
D. Plantation crops	4. Coffee

Codes

	A	B	C	D		A	B	C	D
(a)	1	2	3	4	(b)	2	1	4	3
(c)	3	4	1	2	(d)	4	3	2	1

25. Read the following statements and choose the correct option.

I. Kharif crops require high amounts of water and hence are monsoon crops.

II. Rabi crops are winter crops.

Codes

(a) Only I

(b) Only II

(c) Both I and II

(d) None of the above

26. Identify the important crop grown in below marked state. This state is the largest producer of this crop, due to its climatic condition.

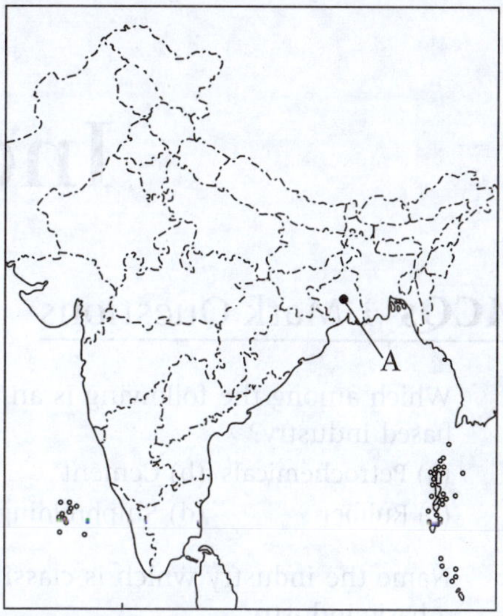

(a) Jute

(b) Oilseeds

(c) Wheat

(d) Cotton

Darken your choice with HB Pencil

1. ⓐ ⓑ ⓒ ⓓ	6. ⓐ ⓑ ⓒ ⓓ	11. ⓐ ⓑ ⓒ ⓓ	16. ⓐ ⓑ ⓒ ⓓ	21. ⓐ ⓑ ⓒ ⓓ	26. ⓐ ⓑ ⓒ ⓓ
2. ⓐ ⓑ ⓒ ⓓ	7. ⓐ ⓑ ⓒ ⓓ	12. ⓐ ⓑ ⓒ ⓓ	17. ⓐ ⓑ ⓒ ⓓ	22. ⓐ ⓑ ⓒ ⓓ	
3. ⓐ ⓑ ⓒ ⓓ	8. ⓐ ⓑ ⓒ ⓓ	13. ⓐ ⓑ ⓒ ⓓ	18. ⓐ ⓑ ⓒ ⓓ	23. ⓐ ⓑ ⓒ ⓓ	
4. ⓐ ⓑ ⓒ ⓓ	9. ⓐ ⓑ ⓒ ⓓ	14. ⓐ ⓑ ⓒ ⓓ	19. ⓐ ⓑ ⓒ ⓓ	24. ⓐ ⓑ ⓒ ⓓ	
5. ⓐ ⓑ ⓒ ⓓ	10. ⓐ ⓑ ⓒ ⓓ	15. ⓐ ⓑ ⓒ ⓓ	20. ⓐ ⓑ ⓒ ⓓ	25. ⓐ ⓑ ⓒ ⓓ	

Chapter 15

Industries

MCQs 1 Mark Questions

1. Which among the following is an agro based industry?
(a) Petrochemicals (b) Cement
(c) Rubber (d) Shipbuilding

2. Name the industry which is classified as a basic industry.
(a) Sugar industry
(b) Machine tool industry
(c) Iron and copper smelting
(d) Paper industry

3. Identify the private sector industry of India.
(a) BHEL
(b) Coal India Ltd
(c) Bharat Electronics Ltd
(d) Godrej Industries

4. Which among the following can be classified as a consumer goods industry?
(a) Petrochemicals
(b) Paper industry
(c) Cement industry
(d) Coal industry

5. The first mechanised paper mill was setup at which place?
(a) Kanpur (b) Barauni
(c) Serampore (d) Murshidabad

6. Identify which was the very first steel plant of India.
(a) Tata Iron and Steel Plant
(b) Rourkela Steel Plant
(c) Indian Iron and Steel Company
(d) Salem Steel Company

7. Which among the following is the largest steel producer in India?
(a) JSW Steel Ltd
(b) Jindal Steel Ltd
(c) Tata Steel Ltd
(d) Ambika Steel Ltd

8. The first cotton textile mill of India was setup at which among the following places?
(a) Ahmedabad (b) Bombay
(c) Jaunpur (d) Kanpur

9. Where was the first jute mill setup in India?
(a) Amritsar (b) Bombay
(c) Kolkata (d) Lucknow

10. Which among the following is related with IT and electronics industry?
(a) Smelting
(b) Business Process Outsourcing
(c) Anti-Dumping
(d) Import Substitution

11. Which among the following is not the sector when industries are categorised based on ownership?
(a) Public (b) Private
(c) Government (d) Cooperative

12. In which year, did the First Industrial Revolution started?
(a) 1740 (b) 1894
(c) 1760 (d) 1902

13. Complete the given analogy based on the textile centres of the countries.
Japan : Osaka :: India : ?
(a) Ahmedabad (b) Mumbai
(c) Bokaro (d) Chennai

14. Identify the incorrectly matched pair based on the industrial centre in India.
(a) Steel – Jamshedpur
(b) Textile – Mumbai
(c) Automobile – Delhi
(d) Sports – Meerut

15. Which among the following is not a Sunrise Industry in India?
(a) Wellness
(b) Hospitality
(c) Knowledge
(d) Steel

16. Which country in the world is the largest producer of tea?
(a) India (b) Ghana
(c) Vietnam (d) China

17. Pick the odd one out about the industries based on input/raw material.
(a) Timber (b) Leather
(c) Sugar (d) Artefacts

18. Identify the incorrectly matched pair based on industry and its product.
(a) Animal based – Wool
(b) Forest based – Turpentine
(c) Metallic based – Cement
(d) Consumer goods – Biscuits

19. The first mechanised paper mill was setup at which place?
(a) Kanpur (b) Serampore
(c) Barauni (d) Murshidabad

MCQs 2 Marks Questions

20. Read the following statements and choose the correct option.
I. Cotton industry is a basic goods industry.
II. Capital goods industry produces those capital goods that are used by other industries.

Codes
(a) Only I (b) Only II
(c) Both I and II (d) None of these

21. Match the following.

List I	List II
A. Public Sector	1. SAIL
B. Private Sector	2. Aditya Birla Group
C. Joint Sector	3. Maruti Udyog Ltd
D. Cooperative Sector	4. AMUL

Codes

	A	B	C	D		A	B	C	D
(a)	1	2	3	4	(b)	2	1	4	3
(c)	3	4	2	1	(d)	4	3	1	2

22. Read the following statements and identifies which ones are true (T) and which ones are false (F).
I. Tyre manufacturing industry is an intermediate goods industry.
II. Paper industry is a forest based industry.
III. Tea and coffee industry is an industrially processed raw material industry.

Codes

	I	II	III		I	II	III
(a)	T	T	T	(b)	F	F	F
(c)	T	F	F	(d)	T	F	T

23. Identify the industry with the help of the description given below.

- It produces goods for direct use of people.
- Sugar, toothpaste, fans are the examples of these industries.

(a) Consumer industries
(b) Small scale industries
(c) Basic industry
(d) Cottage industry

24. Read the following statements and choose the correct option.

I. Markets provides outlet for manufactured products.
II. All the major industrial plants are located on the trunk rail routes.

Codes

(a) Only I (b) Only II
(c) Both I and II (d) None of these

25. Identify the textile with the help of the information given below.

- India is the largest producer and second largest exporter of this material after Bangladesh.
- Most of its mills are located in West Bengal on the banks of Hooghly River.

(a) Sugar
(b) Jute
(c) Petrochemical
(d) Fertilisers

26. Refer to the marking in the given map and identify the famous industry thriving in this region.

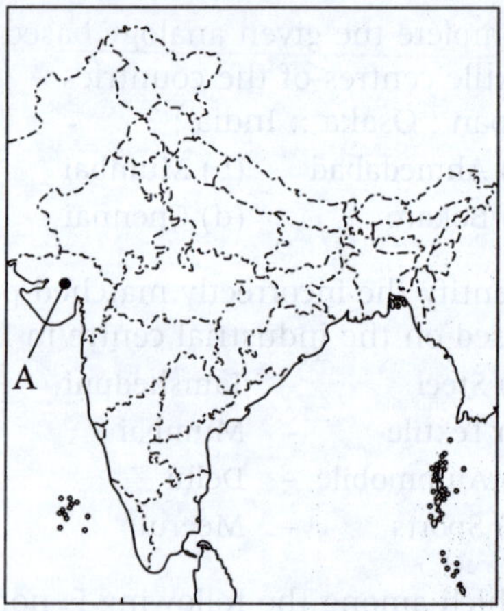

(a) Silk (b) Cotton
(c) Jute (d) Sugar

Darken your choice with HB Pencil

1. ⓐ ⓑ ⓒ ⓓ	6. ⓐ ⓑ ⓒ ⓓ	11. ⓐ ⓑ ⓒ ⓓ	16. ⓐ ⓑ ⓒ ⓓ	21. ⓐ ⓑ ⓒ ⓓ	26. ⓐ ⓑ ⓒ ⓓ
2. ⓐ ⓑ ⓒ ⓓ	7. ⓐ ⓑ ⓒ ⓓ	12. ⓐ ⓑ ⓒ ⓓ	17. ⓐ ⓑ ⓒ ⓓ	22. ⓐ ⓑ ⓒ ⓓ	
3. ⓐ ⓑ ⓒ ⓓ	8. ⓐ ⓑ ⓒ ⓓ	13. ⓐ ⓑ ⓒ ⓓ	18. ⓐ ⓑ ⓒ ⓓ	23. ⓐ ⓑ ⓒ ⓓ	
4. ⓐ ⓑ ⓒ ⓓ	9. ⓐ ⓑ ⓒ ⓓ	14. ⓐ ⓑ ⓒ ⓓ	19. ⓐ ⓑ ⓒ ⓓ	24. ⓐ ⓑ ⓒ ⓓ	
5. ⓐ ⓑ ⓒ ⓓ	10. ⓐ ⓑ ⓒ ⓓ	15. ⓐ ⓑ ⓒ ⓓ	20. ⓐ ⓑ ⓒ ⓓ	25. ⓐ ⓑ ⓒ ⓓ	

Chapter 16

Transport and Communication

MCQs 1 Mark Questions

1. Which modc of transportation links all other mode of transportation?
(a) Roadways (b) Railways
(c) Airways (d) Waterways

2. Identify the city/cities that is/are connected by Golden Quadrilateral Super Highways.
(a) Mumbai (b) Delhi
(c) Kolkata (d) All of these

3. National Highway No 1 runs between Delhi and ....
(a) Jaipur (b) Mumbai
(c) Amritsar (d) Kolkata

4. Which among the following are maintained by Central Public Works Department?
(a) National Highways (b) State Highways
(c) District Roads (d) All of these

5. Which authority is responsible for maintenance of District Roads?
(a) Central Public Works Department
(b) NHAI
(c) Zila Parishad
(d) State Public Works Department

6. Complete the given analogy.
East West Corridor : Silchar and Porbandar :: North-South Corridor : ?
(a) Srinagar and Kanyakumari
(b) Leh and Mumbai
(c) Kashmir and Chennai
(d) Leh and Trivandrum

7. Which of the following roads are all weather roads?
(a) Metalled Roads
(b) Unmetalled Roads
(c) Village Roads
(d) Hill Roads

8. Which among the following is a Tidal Port on the East Coast?
(a) Chennai Port
(b) Kolkata Port
(c) Visakhapatnam Port
(d) Paradip Port

9. Indian transportation is carried out through which inland waterways?
(a) Mandavi
(b) Zuari
(c) Baraks
(d) All of the above

10. Identify the port shown in the picture below. It is the first port established after independence.

(a) Kandla Port
(b) Mumbai Port
(c) Jawharlal Nehru Port
(d) Chennai Port

11. In which state Paradip Port is located?
(a) Bihar (b) West Bengal
(c) Kerala (d) Odisha

12. The first train in India ran between which among the following places?
(a) Kanpur to Agra
(b) Bombay to Thane
(c) Kolkata to Hooghly
(d) Kanpur to Mumbai

13. Identify the material that is not a part of second class mail.
(a) Postcards (b) Books
(c) Newspapers (d) Periodicals

14. When did the first artificial satellite for communication launched?
(a) 1981 (b) 1954
(c) 1957 (d) 1991

15. Which among the following became the first mass medium of circulating information and knowledge among peoples?
(a) Television
(b) Newspapers
(c) Magazines
(d) Radio

MCQs 2 Marks Questions

16. Match the following

List I	List II
A. National Waterway-2	1. Sadiya to Dhubri
B. National Waterway-1	2. Allahabad to Haldia
C. National Waterway-4	3. Krishna Godavari Rivers
D. National Waterway-3	4. West Coast Canal in Kerala

Codes

	A	B	C	D		A	B	C	D
(a)	1	2	3	4	(b)	2	1	4	3
(c)	3	4	2	1	(d)	4	3	1	2

17. There are two statements marked as Assertion (A) and Reason (R). Mark your answer as per the codes given below.

Assertion (A) Waterways are cheapest means of transport.

Reason (R) Waterways are fuel efficient and suitable for carrying heavy and bulky goods.

Codes

(a) Both A and R are true and R is the correct explanation of A
(b) Both A and R are true, but R is not the correct explanation of A
(c) A is true, but R is false
(d) A is false, but R is true

18. Read the following statements and identifies which ones are true (T) and which ones are false (F).

I. Kandla Port is located in Gulf of Kuchchh.
II. Kandla Port is also known as Deendayal Port.
III. Marmagao Port is located in Goa.
IV. Haldia Port is located in West Bengal.

Codes

	I	II	III	IV
(a)	T	T	T	T
(b)	F	F	F	F
(c)	F	T	F	T
(d)	T	F	T	F

19.

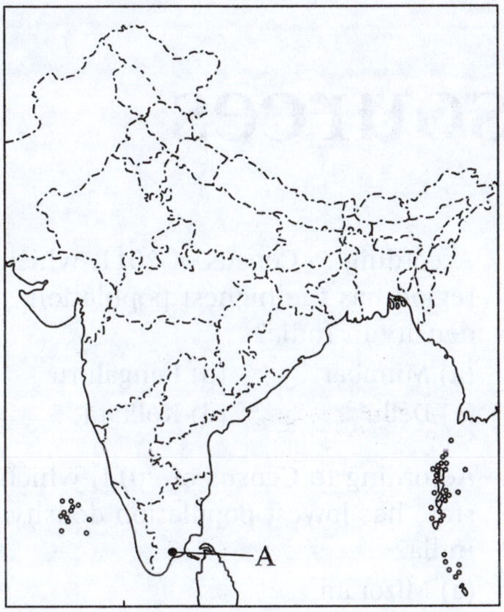

Identify the port which is marked as A in the above map. It is second largest port in Tamil Nadu.

(a) Tuticorin (b) Kandla
(c) Visakhapatnam (d) Cochin

20. Identify the port from the description given below.

- This port is located in Maharashtra.
- It was established to decongest and reduce the burden on Mumbai Port.

(a) Jawaharlal Nehru Port
(b) Kandla
(c) Tuticorin
(d) Paradip

21. Read the following statements and choose the correct option.

I. Satellite communication can be used to send messages to inaccessible areas.

II. E-mail is the most common means of written communication in an organisation.

Codes

(a) Only I
(b) Only II
(c) Both I and II
(d) Neither I nor II

Darken your choice with HB Pencil

1.	ⓐ ⓑ ⓒ ⓓ	5.	ⓐ ⓑ ⓒ ⓓ	9.	ⓐ ⓑ ⓒ ⓓ	13.	ⓐ ⓑ ⓒ ⓓ	17.	ⓐ ⓑ ⓒ ⓓ	21.	ⓐ ⓑ ⓒ ⓓ
2.	ⓐ ⓑ ⓒ ⓓ	6.	ⓐ ⓑ ⓒ ⓓ	10.	ⓐ ⓑ ⓒ ⓓ	14.	ⓐ ⓑ ⓒ ⓓ	18.	ⓐ ⓑ ⓒ ⓓ		
3.	ⓐ ⓑ ⓒ ⓓ	7.	ⓐ ⓑ ⓒ ⓓ	11.	ⓐ ⓑ ⓒ ⓓ	15.	ⓐ ⓑ ⓒ ⓓ	19.	ⓐ ⓑ ⓒ ⓓ		
4.	ⓐ ⓑ ⓒ ⓓ	8.	ⓐ ⓑ ⓒ ⓓ	12.	ⓐ ⓑ ⓒ ⓓ	16.	ⓐ ⓑ ⓒ ⓓ	20.	ⓐ ⓑ ⓒ ⓓ		

Chapter 17

Human Resources

MCQs 1 Mark Questions

1. Which among the following are the ways through which population data is collected in India?
(a) Voting
(b) Census
(c) Tax payments
(d) National Register for citizens

2. .... refers to statistical data relating to population of a region.
(a) Census (b) Demographics
(c) Voting (d) Human Resources

3. When does the positive growth rate of population takes place?
(a) When the death rate is more than birth rate.
(b) When birth rate is more than death rate.
(c) When birth rate and death rate are equal.
(d) When the literacy rate increases.

4. In which year was the first complete census conducted in India?
(a) 1881 (b) 1890 (c) 1900 (d) 1905

5. Identify the factor(s) that determine the extent of concentration of population.
(a) Topography of soil
(b) Availability of water
(c) Temperature
(d) Both (a) and (b)

6. According to Census of 2011, which region has the highest population density in India?
(a) Mumbai (b) Bengaluru
(c) Delhi (d) Kolkata

7. According to Census of 2011, which state has lowest population density in India?
(a) Mizoram
(b) Arunachal Pradesh
(c) Ladakh
(d) Manipur

8. Identify the Union Territory that has the least population density according to 2011 Census of India.
(a) Lakshadweep
(b) Andaman and Nicobar
(c) Puducherry
(d) Daman and Diu

9. Which tool is widely used to analyse the measure of gender balance in a country?
(a) Sex ratio (b) Birth rate
(c) Growth rate (d) Literacy rate

10. Identify the variables used to improve the quality of life.
(a) Literacy rate
(b) Educational development
(c) Healthcare facilities
(d) Both (a) and (b)

11. Which of these states has the highest population of Scheduled Tribes in India?
(a) Madhya Pradesh
(b) Mizoram
(c) Uttar Pradesh
(d) Rajasthan

12. Which among the following is/are the cause(s) of migration from rural areas to urban areas in India?
(a) Poverty
(b) High population pressure on land
(c) Lack of basic infrastructure
(d) All of the above

13. Complete the following analogy.
People who leaves the country: Emigrants : : ? : Immigrants
(a) People who study in a country for short period
(b) People who are tourists
(c) People who arrive in a country
(d) People who are the citizens of a country

MCQs 2 Marks Questions

14. Consider the following statements and choose the correct option.
I. Kerala has the highest literacy rate in India as per census 2011.
II. Crude death rate is number of deaths in a particular month per hundred population in a country.
III. Negative growth rate happens when birth rates and death rates are equal.

Codes
(a) Only I (b) Only II
(c) Only III (d) I and III

15. Read the following statements and choose the correct option.
I. Census is held after every 15 years in India.
II. Natural growth of population is analysed by assessing crude birth and death rates.

Codes
(a) Only I (b) Only II
(c) Both I and II (d) None of these

16. Consider the following statements and choose the correct option.
I. Remittance from International migrants are one of the major sources for foreign exchange.
II. Migrants act as the agents of social change.

Codes
(a) Only I (b) Only II
(c) Both I and II (d) Neither I nor II

17. Match the following.

List I	List II
A. Sex ratio	1. Number of live birth for every 1000 people in a year
B. Life Expectancy	2. Average length of life that a new born is expected to live
C. Birth rate	3. Number of deaths of infants per 1000 of births in a year
D. Infant Mortality	4. Number of females per 1000 males

Codes

	A	B	C	D		A	B	C	D
(a)	2	1	3	4	(b)	1	2	3	4
(c)	4	2	1	3	(d)	3	4	2	1

Darken your choice with HB Pencil

1. ⓐ ⓑ ⓒ ⓓ	4. ⓐ ⓑ ⓒ ⓓ	7. ⓐ ⓑ ⓒ ⓓ	10. ⓐ ⓑ ⓒ ⓓ	13. ⓐ ⓑ ⓒ ⓓ	16. ⓐ ⓑ ⓒ ⓓ
2. ⓐ ⓑ ⓒ ⓓ	5. ⓐ ⓑ ⓒ ⓓ	8. ⓐ ⓑ ⓒ ⓓ	11. ⓐ ⓑ ⓒ ⓓ	14. ⓐ ⓑ ⓒ ⓓ	17. ⓐ ⓑ ⓒ ⓓ
3. ⓐ ⓑ ⓒ ⓓ	6. ⓐ ⓑ ⓒ ⓓ	9. ⓐ ⓑ ⓒ ⓓ	12. ⓐ ⓑ ⓒ ⓓ	15. ⓐ ⓑ ⓒ ⓓ	

Chapter 18

Money and Banking

MCQs 1 Mark Questions

1. Which among the following is an example of digital banking?
   (a) Cheque
   (b) Demand draft
   (c) Deposit form
   (d) ATM card

2. What were the earliest form of objects used as money in India?
   (a) Grains and cattle
   (b) Coins
   (c) Jewels
   (d) Land

3. The Governor of Reserve Bank of India is selected by which of the following?
   (a) The Cabinet
   (b) The President
   (c) The Deputy Governors
   (d) Minister of Corporate Affairs

4. In a Self Help Group most of the decisions regarding savings and loan activities are taken by whom amongst the following?
   (a) Cooperative bank
   (b) Members
   (c) Non-government organisation
   (d) None of the above

5. In rural areas, the main demand for credit is for which purpose?
   (a) Industry
   (b) Crop production
   (c) Irrigation
   (d) Both (b) and (c)

6. Which among the following organisations are authorised to arrange formal sector loans?
   (a) Banks
   (b) Cooperatives
   (c) Moneylenders
   (d) Both (a) and (b)

7. In which year did the demonetisation take place in India?
   (a) 2015
   (b) 2020
   (c) 2016
   (d) 2014

8. Which among the following were the main aim(s) of introducing demonetisation in India?
   (a) To end the corruption.
   (b) To lower the circulation of money in the country.
   (c) To reduce the circulation of fake currency in the country.
   (d) All of the above

9. In India, which organisation has the sole authority to issue currency?
(a) Reserve Bank of India
(b) State Bank of India
(c) Central Government
(d) Finance Ministry

10. The deposits with the bank are known as ....
(a) Advance Deposits (b) Fixed Deposits
(c) Recurring Deposits (d) Demand Deposits

11. In India, how much amount of cash is kept in the form of deposits with the banks?
(a) 10% (b) 15% (c) 20% (d) 50%

12. Who among the following is/are part(s) of informal sources of credit in India?
(a) Moneylenders (b) Traders
(c) Landowners (d) All of these

13. Which bank was previously known as Imperial Bank of India?
(a) Reserve Bank of India
(b) State Bank of India
(c) ICICI Bank
(d) Punjab National Bank

14. In the banking sector, the term CRR stands for which of the following?
(a) Collateral Rising Ratio
(b) Cash Reserve Ratio
(c) Capital Regulation Ratio
(d) Cash Regulation Reserves

15. Identify the public sector bank from the options given below.
(a) IndusInd Bank
(b) HDFC Bank
(c) State Bank of India
(d) ICICI Bank

16. Who among the following issues metallic coins in India?
(a) RBI
(b) Government of India
(c) Banks and Financial institutions
(d) All of the above

MCQs 2 Marks Questions

17. Consider the following statements and choose the correct option.
I. Modern forms of money includes only paper notes.
II. Coins are not considered as modern forms of money.

Codes
(a) Only I
(b) Only II
(c) Both I and II
(d) None of the above

18. Read the following statements and identifies which ones are true (T) and which ones are false (F).
I. Currency is not the generally accepted form of money.
II. Banks do not have to pay an interest on deposits.
III. Banks charge higher rate of interest on loans.
IV. Rate of interest on the loans is the income earned by the banks.

Codes

	I	II	III	IV
(a)	T	T	T	T
(b)	F	T	F	F
(c)	F	T	F	T
(d)	F	F	T	T

19. There are two statements marked as Assertion (A) Reason (R). Mark your answer as per the codes given below.

Assertion (A) Formal sector provides credit at lower rate of interest.

Reason (R) Formal sector is mainly controlled and supervised by RBI.

Codes

(a) Both A and R are true and R is the correct explanation of A

(b) Both A and R are true, but R is not the correct explanation of A

(c) A is true, but R is false

(d) A is false, but R is true

20. Consider the following statements and choose the correct option.

I. Informal sector charges lower rates of interest on loans.

II. Informal sector can lead to increasing debts.

III. Poor households and urban and rural areas depend on informal sector for credit.

Codes

(a) I and II (b) II and III

(c) I and III (d) I, II and III

21. Identify the name of the bank with the help of information given below.

- It is an Indian multinational public sector bank and financial service body.
- It is the largest bank in India.

Codes

(a) Bank of India

(b) Bank of Baroda

(c) State Bank of India

(d) Canara Bank

Darken your choice with HB Pencil

1.	ⓐ ⓑ ⓒ ⓓ	5.	ⓐ ⓑ ⓒ ⓓ	9.	ⓐ ⓑ ⓒ ⓓ	13.	ⓐ ⓑ ⓒ ⓓ	17.	ⓐ ⓑ ⓒ ⓓ	21.	ⓐ ⓑ ⓒ ⓓ
2.	ⓐ ⓑ ⓒ ⓓ	6.	ⓐ ⓑ ⓒ ⓓ	10.	ⓐ ⓑ ⓒ ⓓ	14.	ⓐ ⓑ ⓒ ⓓ	18.	ⓐ ⓑ ⓒ ⓓ		
3.	ⓐ ⓑ ⓒ ⓓ	7.	ⓐ ⓑ ⓒ ⓓ	11.	ⓐ ⓑ ⓒ ⓓ	15.	ⓐ ⓑ ⓒ ⓓ	19.	ⓐ ⓑ ⓒ ⓓ		
4.	ⓐ ⓑ ⓒ ⓓ	8.	ⓐ ⓑ ⓒ ⓓ	12.	ⓐ ⓑ ⓒ ⓓ	16.	ⓐ ⓑ ⓒ ⓓ	20.	ⓐ ⓑ ⓒ ⓓ		

Chapter 19

Constitution and its Features

MCQs 1 Mark Questions

1. Who is the constitutional head of India?
(a) President (b) Prime Minister
(c) Vice-President (d) None of these

2. How many seats were designed for Constituent Assembly?
(a) 552 (b) 389
(c) 401 (d) 250

3. Identify the person who was the Chairman of the Drafting Committee.
(a) Dr BR Ambedkar
(b) Jawaharlal Nehru
(c) Rajendra Prasad
(d) Vallabhbhai Patel

4. The Constitution of India is divided into how many parts?
(a) 24 (b) 22
(c) 21 (d) 23

5. How many schedules are there in the Constitution?
(a) 11 (b) 13
(c) 12 (d) 14

6. Concurrent lists are mentioned in which schedule of the Constitution?
(a) 6 (b) 7
(c) 8 (d) 9

7. Constitutional amendment is mentioned in which part of the Constitution?
(a) Part 18 (b) Part 15
(c) Part 17 (d) Part 20

8. Who among the following put forth the 'Objective Resolution' in the Constituent Assembly?
(a) Rajendra Prasad
(b) Dr BR Ambedkar
(c) Jawaharlal Nehru
(d) Sachchidananda Sinha

9. Who among the following was the constitutional advisor of India?
(a) Dr BR Ambedkar (b) BN Rao
(c) Rajendra Prasad (d) Jawaharlal Nehru

10. The parliamentary system is borrowed from which country?
(a) Canada (b) USA (c) France (d) Britain

11. Election commission is mentioned in which part of the Constitution?
(a) 14 (b) 13 (c) 15 (d) 18

12. Who among the following was not a member of the Drafting Committee of the Constitution?
(a) Mohammad Sadullah
(b) Dr BR Ambedkar
(c) Alladi Krishna Swamy Iyer
(d) Jawaharlal Nehru

13. Who was the Chairman of the Advisory Committee on Fundamental Rights and Minority?

(a) Jawaharlal Nehru (b) BR Ambedkar
(c) BN Rao (d) Sardar Patel

14. The first draft of the Constitution was prepared by whom?

(a) BR Ambedkar (b) Jawaharlal Nehru
(c) Sardar Patel (d) BN Rao

15. In how many days did the Constituent Assembly prepare the Indian Constitution?

(a) 2 years 11 month 18 days (b) 3 years
(c) 4 years (d) 2 years

16. In which of the following countries did the system of judicial review originate?

(a) USA (b) France
(c) Britain (d) Australia

17. The federal system with a strong centre has been borrowed by the Indian Constitution from which country?

(a) USA (b) France
(c) Australia (d) Canada

18. How many articles are there in the Indian Constitution?

(a) 495 (b) 360 (c) 305 (d) 395

19. Identify the incorrectly matched pair.

	Committee		Head
(a)	Drafting Committee	–	BR Ambedkar
(b)	Union Power Committee	–	Jawaharlal Nehru
(c)	Rules of Procedure Committee	–	Rajendra Prasad
(d)	Union Constitution Committee	–	BN Rao

20. In India, the concept of single citizenship is adopted from which country?

(a) UK (b) USA (c) Canada (d) France

21. Which of the following was known as the Provisional Parliament of India?

(a) Indian National Congress
(b) Executive Committee
(c) Drafting Committee
(d) Constituent Assembly

22. The method of impeachment of the President of India is adopted from ....

(a) UK (b) USA
(c) France (d) Pakistan

23. Who among the following was the first Vice-President of the Constituent Assembly?

(a) VT Krishnamachari
(b) HC Mookerjee
(c) BN Rao
(d) Both (a) and (b)

24. Identify the incorrectly matched pair.

	Event/Person		Ideals
(a)	Russian Revolution	–	Socialist principles
(b)	Mahatma Gandhi	–	Strong Centre
(c)	French Revolution	–	Liberty, Equality, Fraternity
(d)	American Constitution	–	Preamble

MCQs 2 Marks Questions

25. Identify the personality from the description given below.

- He was appointed as the temporary President of the Constituent Assembly as he was the eldest member.
- He began a movement for a separate province of Bihar with a small group of others.

(a) Sachchidananda Sinha
(b) Raja Ram Mohan Roy
(c) Shri Ram Krishna Sinha
(d) Raj Kumar Shukla

26. Read the following statements and choose the correct option.

I. Indian Constitution is lengthiest written Constitution.

II. UK written Constitution provided source for Indian Constitution.

Codes

(a) Only I

(b) Only II

(c) Both I and II

(d) None of the above

27. Match the following.

List I (Content)	**List II** (Part)
A. The Union its territory	1. Part III
B. Citizenship	2. Part I
C. Fundamental Rights	3. Part IVA
D. Fundamental Duties	4. Part II

Codes

	A	B	C	D		A	B	C	D
(a)	2	4	1	3	(b)	3	2	4	1
(c)	4	1	3	2	(d)	1	3	2	4

28. There are two statements marked as Assertion (A) and Reason (R). Mark your answer as per the codes given below.

Assertion (A) 42nd Amendment Act is known as Mini Constitution.

Reason (R) It brought local government in India.

Codes

(a) Both A and R are true and R is the correct explanation of A

(b) Both A and R are true, but R is not the correct explanation of A

(c) A is true, but R is false

(d) A is false, but R is true

29. Match the following.

List I (Countries)	**List II** (Borrowed Features)
A. Australia	1. Concurrent list
B. UK	2. Parliamentary government
C. USA	3. Fundamental Rights
D. France	4. Republic

Codes

	A	B	C	D
(a)	2	3	4	1
(b)	3	1	2	4
(c)	4	2	3	2
(d)	1	2	3	4

30. Consider the following statements and choose the correct option.

I. Fundamental Rights Committee was headed by Vallabhbhai Patel.

II. First Speaker of Lok Sabha was GV Mavalankar.

III. Objective Resolution was unanimously adopted on 22nd January, 1947.

Codes

(a) I and II (b) II and III

(c) I and III (d) I, II and III

Darken your choice with HB Pencil

1.	ⓐ ⓑ ⓒ ⓓ	6.	ⓐ ⓑ ⓒ ⓓ	11.	ⓐ ⓑ ⓒ ⓓ	16.	ⓐ ⓑ ⓒ ⓓ	21.	ⓐ ⓑ ⓒ ⓓ	26.	ⓐ ⓑ ⓒ ⓓ
2.	ⓐ ⓑ ⓒ ⓓ	7.	ⓐ ⓑ ⓒ ⓓ	12.	ⓐ ⓑ ⓒ ⓓ	17.	ⓐ ⓑ ⓒ ⓓ	22.	ⓐ ⓑ ⓒ ⓓ	27.	ⓐ ⓑ ⓒ ⓓ
3.	ⓐ ⓑ ⓒ ⓓ	8.	ⓐ ⓑ ⓒ ⓓ	13.	ⓐ ⓑ ⓒ ⓓ	18.	ⓐ ⓑ ⓒ ⓓ	23.	ⓐ ⓑ ⓒ ⓓ	28.	ⓐ ⓑ ⓒ ⓓ
4.	ⓐ ⓑ ⓒ ⓓ	9.	ⓐ ⓑ ⓒ ⓓ	14.	ⓐ ⓑ ⓒ ⓓ	19.	ⓐ ⓑ ⓒ ⓓ	24.	ⓐ ⓑ ⓒ ⓓ	29.	ⓐ ⓑ ⓒ ⓓ
5.	ⓐ ⓑ ⓒ ⓓ	10.	ⓐ ⓑ ⓒ ⓓ	15.	ⓐ ⓑ ⓒ ⓓ	20.	ⓐ ⓑ ⓒ ⓓ	25.	ⓐ ⓑ ⓒ ⓓ	30.	ⓐ ⓑ ⓒ ⓓ

Chapter 20

Fundamental Rights and DPSPs

MCQs 1 Mark Questions

1. In which part of the Indian Constitution the Fundamental Rights are provided?
(a) Part IV (b) Part II
(c) Part III (d) Part V

2. Fundamental Rights come under which articles?
(a) 12 – 35 (b) 36 – 51
(c) 5 – 11 (d) 51A

3. Which part of the Indian Constitution is called Magna Carta?
(a) Part I (b) Part II
(c) Part III (d) Part IV

4. Article 19 to Article 22 of Indian Constitution grant which of the following rights?
(a) Right to Life (b) Right to Property
(c) Right to Equality (d) Right to Freedom

5. Which among the following articles of the Constitution of India abolishes untouchability?
(a) Article 12 (b) Article 19
(c) Article 17 (d) Article 18

6. In the Constitution of India, how many Fundamental Rights are mentioned?
(a) 8 (b) 5 (c) 9 (d) 6

7. Article 21A of the Constitution of India provides the Right to ....
(a) equality
(b) education
(c) work
(d) privacy

8. How many freedoms are granted by the Article 19 'Right to Freedom'?
(a) 6 (b) 5 (c) 7 (d) 4

9. The Concept of Welfare State is described in which parts of the Indian Constitution?
(a) DPSP
(b) Citizenship
(c) Fundamental Rights
(d) Fundamental Duties

10. Which one of the following is not an objective of the DPSP?
(a) To establish a secular state
(b) To establish a religion state
(c) To establish a welfare state
(d) None of the above

11. Articles (14-18) deals with which subject in our Constitution?
(a) Right to Equality
(b) Protection from Arrests
(c) Right to Religion
(d) Freedom of Movement

12. Which among the following is the Gandhian Principle of the DPSPs?
(a) Free and compulsory education for all
(b) Promotion of cottage industries
(c) Protecting monuments
(d) Prevent concentration of wealth

13. How many types of writs can be issued by the Supreme Court under Article 32?
(a) 5 (b) 6 (c) 7 (d) 8

14. From which country has the Indian Constitution borrowed DPSP?
(a) USA (b) Ireland
(c) France (d) Australia

15. Which amendment deleted the Right to Property from Fundamental Rights?
(a) 44th (b) 42nd
(c) 43rd (d) 46th

16. Which part of the Constitution is called the soul of the Constitution?
(a) Preamble
(b) DPSP
(c) Fundamental Rights
(d) Fundamental Duties

17. From the given options, choose which one is justifiable in courts.
(a) DPSP
(b) Preamble
(c) Fundamental Rights
(d) Fundamental Duties

18. Which Constitutional Amendment Act was passed to provide compulsory education to children between the ages of 6 to 14?
(a) 42nd (b) 44th (c) 97th (d) 86th

19. Who among the following is the guardian of Fundamental Rights?
(a) Judiciary (b) Legislature
(c) Executive (d) Political parties

20. Which of the following statements is the correct explanation of the Right to Constitutional Remedies?
(a) It provides solutions to an individuals issues.
(b) It contains the remedies with respect to any Fundamental Rights violation.
(c) Both (a) and (b)
(d) None of the above

MCQs 2 Marks Questions

21. Consider the following statements regarding Fundamental Rights and choose the correct option.
I. Fundamental Rights are justifiable and enforceable in courts.
II. Supreme Court issues writs to enforce Fundamental Rights under Article 32.
III. The President protects the Fundamental Rights of Indian citizens.

Codes
(a) I and II
(b) II and III
(c) I and III
(d) All of the above

22. There are two statements marked as Assertion (A) and Reason (R). Mark your answer as per the codes given below.

Assertion (A) DPSP was originally part of Indian Constitution.

Reason (R) It is mentioned in Part IVA of Indian Constitution.

Codes
(a) Both A and R are true and R is the correct explanation of A
(b) Both A and R are true, but R is not the correct explanation of A
(c) A is true, but R is false
(d) A is false, but R is true

23. Read the following statements and identifies which ones are true (T) which ones are false (F).

I. Fundamental Rights are dealt in from Articles 12-35.

II. District Court deals with Fundamental Rights

III. Right to Religion is part of Fundamental Rights.

IV. Fundamental Duties are also mentioned in Part III.

Codes

	I	II	III	IV		I	II	III	IV
(a)	T	T	T	F	(b)	F	F	F	F
(c)	T	F	T	F	(d)	T	F	F	F

24. Consider the following statements and choose the correct option.

I. Right to Property is a Fundamental Right.

II. Right to Privacy is mentioned in Article 21.

Codes

(a) Only I
(b) Only II
(c) Both I and II
(d) None of the above

25. Identify the part of Indian Constitution from the description given below.

- This part gives directions to the State regarding policies.
- Right to Education for ages 6-14 was included as Fundamental Rights by this part.

(a) Part-IV (DPSP)
(b) Part IVA (Fundamental Duties)
(c) Part III (Fundamental Rights)
(d) Part II (Citizenship)

26. Match the following.

	List I (Fundamental Rights)		List II (Articles)
A.	Right to Equality	1.	14-18
B.	Right to Freedom	2.	19-22
C.	Right against Exploitation	3.	23-24
D.	Cultural and Education Right	4.	29-30

Codes

	A	B	C	D
(a)	1	2	3	4
(b)	3	1	2	4
(c)	2	4	1	3
(d)	4	1	3	2

Darken your choice with HB Pencil

1. ⓐ ⓑ ⓒ ⓓ	6. ⓐ ⓑ ⓒ ⓓ	11. ⓐ ⓑ ⓒ ⓓ	16. ⓐ ⓑ ⓒ ⓓ	21. ⓐ ⓑ ⓒ ⓓ	26. ⓐ ⓑ ⓒ ⓓ
2. ⓐ ⓑ ⓒ ⓓ	7. ⓐ ⓑ ⓒ ⓓ	12. ⓐ ⓑ ⓒ ⓓ	17. ⓐ ⓑ ⓒ ⓓ	22. ⓐ ⓑ ⓒ ⓓ	
3. ⓐ ⓑ ⓒ ⓓ	8. ⓐ ⓑ ⓒ ⓓ	13. ⓐ ⓑ ⓒ ⓓ	18. ⓐ ⓑ ⓒ ⓓ	23. ⓐ ⓑ ⓒ ⓓ	
4. ⓐ ⓑ ⓒ ⓓ	9. ⓐ ⓑ ⓒ ⓓ	14. ⓐ ⓑ ⓒ ⓓ	19. ⓐ ⓑ ⓒ ⓓ	24. ⓐ ⓑ ⓒ ⓓ	
5. ⓐ ⓑ ⓒ ⓓ	10. ⓐ ⓑ ⓒ ⓓ	15. ⓐ ⓑ ⓒ ⓓ	20. ⓐ ⓑ ⓒ ⓓ	25. ⓐ ⓑ ⓒ ⓓ	

Chapter 21

Our Government (Executive, Legislature and Judiciary)

MCQs 1 Mark Questions

1. Which part of the Indian Constitution deals with the Union Government?
(a) Part IV (b) Part II
(c) Part V (d) Part VI

2. Who among the following receives the President's resignation letter?
(a) Vice-President
(b) Chief Justice of India
(c) Prime Minister
(d) Governor

3. What is the minimum age required for the election as President?
(a) 30 (b) 40 (c) 35 (d) 32

4. Who has the supreme command over the Defence Forces in India?
(a) Prime Minister
(b) President
(c) Chief of Defence Staff
(d) Chief of Army

5. Which among the following administers oath to the President of India?
(a) Vice-President
(b) Prime Minister
(c) Chief Justice of India
(d) Former President

6. In the Constitution of India, which Article deals with the Vice-President?
(a) Article 50 (b) Article 89
(c) Article 90 (d) Article 63

7. The Vice-President is ex officio Chairman of ....
(a) House of People
(b) Council of States
(c) Election Commission
(d) University Grant Commission

8. Choose the incorrectly matched pair
(a) Governor – Head of State
(b) Prime Minister – Head of Government
(c) Vice-President – Chairman of Council of States
(d) Defence Minister – Commander of Armed Forces

9. Who among the following presents the Budget?
(a) President (b) Finance Minister
(c) Prime Minister (d) None of these

10. Who is the Chancellor of Central universities?
(a) Vice-President (b) President
(c) Governor (d) Prime Minister

11. Who among the following is appoints the Prime Minister of India?
(a) President of India
(b) Chief Justice of India
(c) Speaker of the Lok Sabha
(d) Vice-President of India

12. What is the minimum age for holding office in the Lok Sabha?
(a) 18 years (b) 21 years
(c) 25 years (d) 30 years

13. How many sessions of the Lok Sabha take place in a year?
(a) 2 (b) 3
(c) 4 (d) 5

14. What is the another name of the Council of States?
(a) Lok Sabha
(b) Rajya Sabha
(c) Parliament
(d) Adhoc Committee

15. What is the maximum strength (number of members) of the Rajya Sabha?
(a) 220 (b) 235
(c) 238 (d) 250

16. As per the Constitution of India, what is the maximum strength of the Lok Sabha?
(a) 530 (b) 540
(c) 550 (d) 552

17. Who among the following is the presiding officer of the Lok Sabha?
(a) President
(b) Vice-President
(c) Speaker of Lok Sabha
(d) Prime Minister

18. What is the tenure of the elected members of Rajya Sabha?
(a) 2 years (b) 4 years
(c) 6 years (d) 8 years

19. Complete the given analogy.
Rajya Sabha : : Chairman : Lok Sabha : ?
(a) Deputy Speaker
(b) Leader of House
(c) Vice-President
(d) Speaker

20. Identify the person in the picture given below who was the first Speaker of Lok Sabha.

(a) KS Hegde (b) Hukam Singh
(c) MA Ayyangar (d) Ganesh Mavlankar

MCQs 2 Marks Questions

21. Consider the following statements regarding the President and choose the correct option.
I. The President is the Head of State.
II. The President has powers to pardon.
III. The President protects the Fundamental Rights of Indian Citizens.

Codes
(a) I and II (b) II and III
(c) I and III (d) All of these

22. There are two statements marked as Assertion (A) and Reason (R). Mark your answer as per the codes given below.

Assertion (A) Parliament is composed of Lok Sabha, Rajya Sabha and the President.

Reason (R) President takes part in Parliament proceedings.

Codes

(a) Both A and R are true and R is the correct explanation of A

(b) Both A and R are true, but R is not the correct explanation of A

(c) A is true, but R is false

(d) A is false, but R is true

23. Match the following.

List I (Union subjects)	**List II** (Articles)
A. Supreme Court	1. Article 124
B. Comptroller and Auditor General	2. Article 148
C. Parliament	3. Article 79

Codes

	A	B	C		A	B	C
(a)	1	2	3	(b)	2	1	3
(c)	1	3	2	(d)	3	2	1

24. Read the following statements and choose the correct option.

I. Attorney General of India is elected by people.

II. Attorney General is the chief legal advisor of the Government of India.

Codes

(a) Only I (b) Only II

(c) Both I and II (d) Neither I nor II

25. Identify the House of Indian Parliament from the below given description.

- It has a maximum membership of 250.
- Vice-President is ex-officio Chairman of this house.

(a) Rajya Sabha

(b) Lok Sabha

(c) Both (a) and (b)

(d) None of the above

26. Read the following statements and identifies which ones are true (T) and which ones are false (F).

I. President is elected by people.

II. Vice-President is elected by MPs and MLAs.

III. Supreme Court Judges retire at the age of 65 years.

IV. Chief Justice of India is appointed by the Prime Minister.

Codes

	I	II	III	IV
(a)	T	T	T	F
(b)	F	T	T	F
(c)	T	F	T	F
(d)	T	F	F	F

Darken your choice with HB Pencil

1.	ⓐ ⓑ ⓒ ⓓ	6.	ⓐ ⓑ ⓒ ⓓ	11.	ⓐ ⓑ ⓒ ⓓ	16.	ⓐ ⓑ ⓒ ⓓ	21.	ⓐ ⓑ ⓒ ⓓ	26.	ⓐ ⓑ ⓒ ⓓ
2.	ⓐ ⓑ ⓒ ⓓ	7.	ⓐ ⓑ ⓒ ⓓ	12.	ⓐ ⓑ ⓒ ⓓ	17.	ⓐ ⓑ ⓒ ⓓ	22.	ⓐ ⓑ ⓒ ⓓ		
3.	ⓐ ⓑ ⓒ ⓓ	8.	ⓐ ⓑ ⓒ ⓓ	13.	ⓐ ⓑ ⓒ ⓓ	18.	ⓐ ⓑ ⓒ ⓓ	23.	ⓐ ⓑ ⓒ ⓓ		
4.	ⓐ ⓑ ⓒ ⓓ	9.	ⓐ ⓑ ⓒ ⓓ	14.	ⓐ ⓑ ⓒ ⓓ	19.	ⓐ ⓑ ⓒ ⓓ	24.	ⓐ ⓑ ⓒ ⓓ		
5.	ⓐ ⓑ ⓒ ⓓ	10.	ⓐ ⓑ ⓒ ⓓ	15.	ⓐ ⓑ ⓒ ⓓ	20.	ⓐ ⓑ ⓒ ⓓ	25.	ⓐ ⓑ ⓒ ⓓ		

Chapter 22

Panchayati Raj Institutions

MCQs 1 Mark Questions

1. Which schedule of the Indian Constitution deals with the Panchayati Raj Institutions?
   (a) Schedule IV
   (b) Schedule II
   (c) Schedule XI
   (d) Schedule V

2. Which amendment added the Panchayati Raj Institutions in the Constitution of India?
   (a) 123rd Constitutional Amendment
   (b) 44th Constitutional Amendment
   (c) 5th Constitutional Amendment
   (d) 73rd Constitutional Amendment

3. How many posts are reserved for women in the Panchayati Raj system?
   (a) 1/3 (b) 2/3
   (c) 1/2 (d) All posts

4. What is the minimum age required for the elections in Panchayat?
   (a) 30 (b) 25
   (c) 21 (d) 18

5. When was the Panchayati Raj system implemented in India?
   (a) 1956 (b) 1992
   (c) 1998 (d) 2000

6. Gram Panchayat is elected by which of the following peoples?
   (a) All voters of Village
   (b) Zila Parishad Members
   (c) MLA
   (d) President

7. Which of the following is not a level in Panchayati Raj Institutions?
   (a) Gram Panchayat (b) Zila Parishad
   (c) Block Panchayat (d) State Panchayat

8. The elections of Panchayat are conducted by ....
   (a) Election Commission of India
   (b) State Election Commission
   (c) High Court
   (d) State Government

9. Which of the following committees recommended the Panchayati Raj system?
   (a) Balwant Rai Mehta Committee
   (b) JPV Committee
   (c) Punchhi Committee
   (d) Sarakaria Committee

10. 73rd Constitutional Amendment added which part to the Indian Constitution?
    (a) X (b) XI
    (c) VII (d) IX

11. Who among the following is the head of the Zila Parishad?

(a) District Judge
(b) Mayor
(c) Adhyaksha/President
(d) Pradhan

12. Identify the incorrectly matched pair

(a) Pradhan – Head of Panchayat
(b) Zila Parishad – District Panchayat
(c) Term of Panchayat – 4 years
(d) None of the above

13. What is the method of election at block and district level of Panchayat?

(a) Direct election (b) Nomination
(c) Indirect election (d) Both (a) and (b)

14. Which of the following committees is not related to Panchayati Raj Institutions?

(a) Balwant Rai Mehta Committee
(b) Ashok Mehta Committee
(c) GVK Rao Committee
(d) Sarkari Commission

15. Who is known as the father of the Panchayati Raj system in India?

(a) Mahatma Gandhi
(b) Subhash Chandra Bose
(c) Balwant Rai Mehta
(d) Indira Gandhi

16. Which article in DPSP talks about Panchayat?

(a) Article 49 (b) Article 39
(c) Article 47 (d) Article 40

17. When is National Panchayati Raj Day celebrated in India?

(a) 26th January
(b) 30th March
(c) 24th April
(d) None of the above

18. Which was the first state to introduce Panchayats in India?

(a) Uttar Pradesh
(b) Bihar
(c) Karnataka
(d) Rajasthan

19. How many members are nominated in Gram Sabha?

(a) 10
(b) 2
(c) 5
(d) Nomination is not done

MCQs 2 Marks Questions

20. Consider the following statements regarding the Panchayat and choose the correct option.

I. The District Judge is the Head of Panchayat.
II. The President has powers to dissolve the Panchayat.
III. The Panchayat protects the Fundamental Rights of Villagers.

Codes

(a) I and II (b) II and III
(c) I and III (d) None of these

21. There are two statements marked as Assertion (A) and Reason (R). Mark your answer as per the codes given below.

Assertion (A) Panchayat is composed of Zila Parishad, Block Parishad and Gram Panchayat.

Reason (R) Panchayati Raj Institutions are three tier in India.

Codes

(a) Both A and R are true and R is the correct explanation of A
(b) Both A and R are true, but R is not the correct explanation of A
(c) A is true, but R is false
(d) A is false, but R is true

22. Read the following statements and identifies which ones are true (T) and which ones are false (F).

I. Every member of the Panchayat is appointed by the President.

II. A member of Panchayat retires after 5 years of term.

III. Person of any state can be appointed as a Gram Panchayat member.

Codes

	I	II	III		I	II	III
(a)	T	T	T	(b)	F	F	F
(c)	F	T	F	(d)	T	F	F

23. There are two statements marked as Assertion (A) and Reason (R). Mark your answer as per the codes given below.

Assertion (A) Block Panchayat makes development plans at block level.

Reason (R) Block Panchayat is elected at Block level.

Codes

(a) Both A and R are true and R is the correct explanation of A

(b) Both A and R are true, but R is not the correct explanation of A

(c) A is true, but R is false

(d) A is false, but B is true.

24. Read the following statements and choose the correct option.

I. Zila Parishad is elected by people.

II. Panchayat discusses the court cases at Village level.

Codes

(a) Only I (b) Only II

(c) Both I and II (d) None of these

25. Identify the level of Panchayat with the given below description.

- It is an intermediate level of Panchayati System.
- Its members are indirectly elected by Village Panchayat members.

(a) Block Panchayat (b) Zila Parishad

(c) Both (a) and (b) (d) Gram Samiti

26. Read the following statements and identifies which ones are true (T) and which ones are false (F).

I. Governor is responsible for elections of Panchayats.

II. State Finance Commission reviews finances of Panchayats.

III. Lok Adalat is a part of Panchayat.

IV. Oath to Panchayat members is administered by the President.

Codes

	I	II	III	IV		I	II	III	IV
(a)	T	T	T	F	(b)	F	T	T	F
(c)	T	F	T	F	(d)	F	T	F	F

27. Match the following.

List I (Committee)	**List II** (Head)
A. Zila Parishad	1. Panch
B. Panchayat President	2. Sarpanch
C. Panchayat Samiti	3. District Panchayat
D. Member of the Panchayat	4. Block Panchayat

Codes

	A	B	C	D		A	B	C	D
(a)	1	2	3	4	(b)	1	2	4	5
(c)	1	3	2	4	(d)	3	2	4	1

Darken your choice with HB Pencil

1.	ⓐ ⓑ ⓒ ⓓ	6.	ⓐ ⓑ ⓒ ⓓ	11.	ⓐ ⓑ ⓒ ⓓ	16.	ⓐ ⓑ ⓒ ⓓ	21.	ⓐ ⓑ ⓒ ⓓ	26.	ⓐ ⓑ ⓒ ⓓ
2.	ⓐ ⓑ ⓒ ⓓ	7.	ⓐ ⓑ ⓒ ⓓ	12.	ⓐ ⓑ ⓒ ⓓ	17.	ⓐ ⓑ ⓒ ⓓ	22.	ⓐ ⓑ ⓒ ⓓ	27.	ⓐ ⓑ ⓒ ⓓ
3.	ⓐ ⓑ ⓒ ⓓ	8.	ⓐ ⓑ ⓒ ⓓ	13.	ⓐ ⓑ ⓒ ⓓ	18.	ⓐ ⓑ ⓒ ⓓ	23.	ⓐ ⓑ ⓒ ⓓ		
4.	ⓐ ⓑ ⓒ ⓓ	9.	ⓐ ⓑ ⓒ ⓓ	14.	ⓐ ⓑ ⓒ ⓓ	19.	ⓐ ⓑ ⓒ ⓓ	24.	ⓐ ⓑ ⓒ ⓓ		
5.	ⓐ ⓑ ⓒ ⓓ	10.	ⓐ ⓑ ⓒ ⓓ	15.	ⓐ ⓑ ⓒ ⓓ	20.	ⓐ ⓑ ⓒ ⓓ	25.	ⓐ ⓑ ⓒ ⓓ		

Chapter 23

Election and Political Parties

MCQs 1 Mark Questions

1. Which part of the Indian Constitution deals with elections?
(a) Part IV (b) Part II
(c) Part XV (d) Part V

2. Who among the following receives the Election Commissioner's resignation letter?
(a) President
(b) Chief Justice of India
(c) Prime Minister
(d) Governor

3. How many members are there in the Election Commission of India?
(a) 6 (b) 4
(c) 3 (d) 2

4. Who among the following appoint the Chief Election Commissioner of India?
(a) Vice-President
(b) Prime Minister
(c) Chief Justice of India
(d) President

5. Election Commission of India recognises which of the following parties?
(a) National Political Party
(b) State Political Party
(c) Both (a) and (b)
(d) Panchayat Level Political Party

6. Election Commission of India conducts elections for which among the following?
(a) State Assembly (b) MPs
(c) President (d) All of these

7. Identify the incorrectly matched pair.
(a) Election of President – Electoral College
(b) Prime Minister – Chosen by winning Party MPs
(c) Vice-President – Electoral College
(d) Governor – State Assembly

8. Who among the following was the first Chief Election Commissioner of India?
(a) Sardar Patel
(b) Sukumar Sen
(c) C Rajagopalachari
(d) None of the above

9. How many national parties are there in India?
(a) 8 (b) 10
(c) 20 (d) 7

10. Which of the following is not a national party?
(a) Samajwadi Party(SP)
(b) Bharatiya Janata Party (BJP)
(c) Bahujan Samaj Party (BSP)
(d) Indian National Congress (INC)

11. The Election Commission of India consists which of the following?
(a) Chief Election Commissioner
(b) Deputy Election Commissioner
(c) Both (a) and (b)
(d) Chief Justice of India

12. Which of the following is related to elections in India?
(a) Representation of People's Act, 1951
(b) 42nd Constitutional Amendment Act
(c) Right to Liberty
(d) Verma Commission

13. In India, which system is followed for elections in the House of People?
(a) Proportional System
(b) First Past the Post electoral system
(c) Single Voting System
(d) Both (a) and (b)

14. When was the Election Commission established for the first time?
(a) 25th January, 1950
(b) 26th January, 1950
(c) 25th January, 1947
(d) 25th January, 1951

15. Complete the given analogy.
Rajya Sabha : Election Commission of India : : Panchayat : ?
(a) Governor
(b) Chief Secretary
(c) PMO
(d) State Election Commission

16. What is the full form of EPIC ?
(a) Electoral Picture Identity Card
(b) Elector's Photo Identity Card
(c) Electricity Card of Proper Identity
(d) None of the above

MCQs 2 Marks Questions

17. Consider the following statements regarding the Election Commission of India and choose the correct option.
I. It is a constitutional body.
II. The President appoints the Election Commissioner.
III. The Election Commission conducts elections for Panchayat.

Codes
(a) I and II (b) II and III
(c) I and III (d) All of these

18. There are two statements marked as Assertion (A) and Reason (R). Mark your answer as per the codes given below.

Assertion (A) A national party is recognised by the Election Commission.

Reason (R) A national party is one which has had a Prime Minister for 3 or more times.

Codes
(a) Both A and R are true and R is the correct explanation of A
(b) Both A and R are true, but R is not the correct explanation of A
(c) A is true, but R is false
(d) A is false, but R is true

19. There are two statements marked as Assertion (A) and Reason (R). Mark your answer as per the codes given below.

Assertion (A) A national party only fights elections for Parliament houses.

Reason (R) Nomination to Parliament is done by the President.

Codes

(a) Both A and R are true and R is the correct explanation of A

(b) Both A and R are true, but R is not the correct explanation of A

(c) A is true, but R is false

(d) A is false, but R is true

20. Consider the following statements regarding the Comptroller and Auditor General of India and choose the correct option.

I. Representation of People's Act gives power to the Election Commission related to elections.

II. The State Election Commissioner is appointed by the President.

III. The Election Commissioner has the right to sit in Parliament.

Codes

(a) I and II

(b) II and III

(c) I and III

(d) All of the above

21. Read the following statements and choose the correct option.

I. A state party of India is elected by people of state.

II. President oversees functions of elections.

Codes

(a) Only I (b) Only II

(c) I and II (d) None of these

22. Identify the Election Commission with the help of the information given below.

- Its chief is appointed by the Governor.
- Tenure of Chief Election Commissioner is of 5 years.

(a) Election Commission of India

(b) State Election Commission

(c) Both (a) and (b)

(d) None of the above

23. Read the following statements and identifies which ones are true (T) and which ones are false (F).

I. Election Commissioner is removed in the same manner as of the Supreme Court Judge.

II. Vice-President's election is not conducted by EC.

III. Panchayat election is done by the State Election Commission.

Codes

	I	II	III
(a)	T	T	T
(b)	F	T	T
(c)	T	F	T
(d)	T	F	F

Darken your choice with HB Pencil

1.	ⓐ ⓑ ⓒ ⓓ	5.	ⓐ ⓑ ⓒ ⓓ	9.	ⓐ ⓑ ⓒ ⓓ	13.	ⓐ ⓑ ⓒ ⓓ	17.	ⓐ ⓑ ⓒ ⓓ	21.	ⓐ ⓑ ⓒ ⓓ
2.	ⓐ ⓑ ⓒ ⓓ	6.	ⓐ ⓑ ⓒ ⓓ	10.	ⓐ ⓑ ⓒ ⓓ	14.	ⓐ ⓑ ⓒ ⓓ	18.	ⓐ ⓑ ⓒ ⓓ	22.	ⓐ ⓑ ⓒ ⓓ
3.	ⓐ ⓑ ⓒ ⓓ	7.	ⓐ ⓑ ⓒ ⓓ	11.	ⓐ ⓑ ⓒ ⓓ	15.	ⓐ ⓑ ⓒ ⓓ	19.	ⓐ ⓑ ⓒ ⓓ	23.	ⓐ ⓑ ⓒ ⓓ
4.	ⓐ ⓑ ⓒ ⓓ	8.	ⓐ ⓑ ⓒ ⓓ	12.	ⓐ ⓑ ⓒ ⓓ	16.	ⓐ ⓑ ⓒ ⓓ	20.	ⓐ ⓑ ⓒ ⓓ		

Chapter 24

Science and Technology

MCQs 1 Mark Questions

1. Which of the following is not a storage device?

(a) Pen Drive (b) Hard Drive
(c) Compact Disk (d) Modern

2. The aviation fuel which is used in the engines of jet aeroplanes is ....

(a) diesel (b) kerosene
(c) petrol (d) CNG

3. What material is mostly used in making of aeroplanes?

(a) Carbon Alloy (b) Steel
(c) Iron (d) Aluminium

4. Which among the following was the first Indian satellite launched to space?

(a) Chandrayaan
(b) Mangalyaan
(c) Aryabhatta
(d) Bhaskara

5. Agni-V Missile is developed by which organisation?

(a) ISRO (b) DRDO
(c) Airforce India (d) HAL

6. Which among the following is not an Indian Missile?

(a) Astra (b) Agni
(c) Ghazi (d) Nag

7. Which space vehicle was sent to Mars by India?

(a) Chandrayaan (b) Mangalyaan
(c) Gaganyaan (d) Shukrayaan

8. When did the Indian Space Research Organisation launch the first space vehicle?

(a) 1962 (b) 1969
(c) 1983 (d) 1995

9. Which is the first tactical surface-to-surface missile of India?

(a) Akash (b) Trishul
(c) Nag (d) Prithvi

10. Identify the incorrectly matched pair.

(a) Agni – Surface-to-Surface
(b) Nag – Anti-tank
(c) Prithvi – Surface to surface
(d) Astra – Surface to air

11. How many types of antibodies are there?

(a) Five (b) Three
(c) Two (d) Four

12. NISAR is a joint Earth-observing mission between the Indian Space Research Organisation (ISRO) and ....

(a) NASA
(b) ESA
(c) JAXA
(d) ROSCOSMOS

13. What is the life-span of Human RBCs?
(a) 115 days approx (b) 200 days approx
(c) 300 days approx (d) 220 days approx

14. Chandrayaan Mission consists of which of the following?
(a) Lunar orbiter
(b) Lander Vikram
(c) Robotic lunar rover Pragyan
(d) All of the above

15. Gaganyaan Mission envisages capability to demonstrate which of the following?
(a) Human space flight
(b) Payload delivery
(c) Satellite launch
(d) Moon landing

16. Which shuttle was the first to send a human to the Moon?
(a) Apollo 11 (b) Artemis
(c) Chandrayaan (d) Gaganyaan

17. Identify the name of launch vehicle which is used for the Gaganyaan Mission.
(a) PSLV (b) SLV-3
(c) GSLV (d) ICBM

18. Which was the first privately owned company to send a mission to space?
(a) Dragon (b) Tesla
(c) NASA (d) SpaceX

19. Hyperloop technology is related to which of the following?
(a) Space Flight
(b) Moon Mission
(c) High Speed Transportation System
(d) Missile Technology

20. BrahMos Supersonic missile has been built with collaboration of which of the following countries?
(a) USA (b) Mongolia
(c) Russia (d) China

21. Which country has/have Missile Defence systems?
(a) Israel (b) United States
(c) India (d) All of these

MCQs 2 Marks Questions

22. There are two statements marked as Assertion (A) and Reason (R). Mark your answer as per the codes given below.
Assertion (A) GSLV is owned by ISRO.
Reason (R) Both ISRO and NASA have developed GSLV together.
Codes
(a) Both A and R are true and R is the correct explanation of A
(b) Both A and R are true, but R is not the correct explanation of A
(c) A is true, but R is false
(d) A is false, but R is true

23. Read the following statements and identifies which ones are true (T) and which ones are false (F).
I. ICBM stands for Inter-Continental Ballistic Missile.
II. Surya Missile is an ICBM.
III. ICBMs can not deliver nuclear weapons.
Codes

	I	II	III		I	II	III
(a)	T	T	T	(b)	F	F	F
(c)	T	T	F	(d)	T	F	F

24. Match the following.

List I (Diseases)	**List II** (Deficiency of Vitamin)
A. Scurvy	1. Vitamin C
B. Beri-Beri	2. Vitamin B
C. Night Blindness	3. Vitamin A
D. Rickets	4. Vitamin D

Codes

	A	B	C	D
(a)	1	2	3	4
(b)	2	1	3	4
(c)	4	3	2	1
(d)	3	4	1	2

25. Consider the following statements regarding the Gaganyaan Mission of India and choose the correct option.

I. It is being developed by ISRO.

II. It will be India's first mission to the Moon.

III. It will test the capability of sending humans to space.

Codes

(a) I and II (b) II and III

(c) I and III (d) All of these

26. Read the following statements and choose the correct option.

I. APJ Abdul Kalam is known as the Missile Man of India.

II. He was involved in development of the Agni Missile system.

Codes

(a) Only I

(b) Only II

(c) Both I and II

(d) None of the above

27. Read the following statements and identifies which ones are true (T) and which ones are false (F).

I. Wi-fi is faster than Li-fi.

II. Blockchain technology is not useful in banking.

III. Ministry of Defence develops Missiles in India.

IV. The Indian Navigation system is called NavIC.

Codes

	I	II	III	IV
(a)	T	T	T	F
(b)	F	T	T	F
(c)	T	F	T	F
(d)	F	F	F	T

Darken your choice with HB Pencil

1. ⓐ ⓑ ⓒ ⓓ	6. ⓐ ⓑ ⓒ ⓓ	11. ⓐ ⓑ ⓒ ⓓ	16. ⓐ ⓑ ⓒ ⓓ	21. ⓐ ⓑ ⓒ ⓓ	26. ⓐ ⓑ ⓒ ⓓ
2. ⓐ ⓑ ⓒ ⓓ	7. ⓐ ⓑ ⓒ ⓓ	12. ⓐ ⓑ ⓒ ⓓ	17. ⓐ ⓑ ⓒ ⓓ	22. ⓐ ⓑ ⓒ ⓓ	27. ⓐ ⓑ ⓒ ⓓ
3. ⓐ ⓑ ⓒ ⓓ	8. ⓐ ⓑ ⓒ ⓓ	13. ⓐ ⓑ ⓒ ⓓ	18. ⓐ ⓑ ⓒ ⓓ	23. ⓐ ⓑ ⓒ ⓓ	
4. ⓐ ⓑ ⓒ ⓓ	9. ⓐ ⓑ ⓒ ⓓ	14. ⓐ ⓑ ⓒ ⓓ	19. ⓐ ⓑ ⓒ ⓓ	24. ⓐ ⓑ ⓒ ⓓ	
5. ⓐ ⓑ ⓒ ⓓ	10. ⓐ ⓑ ⓒ ⓓ	15. ⓐ ⓑ ⓒ ⓓ	20. ⓐ ⓑ ⓒ ⓓ	25. ⓐ ⓑ ⓒ ⓓ	

Chapter 25

Sports

MCQs 1 Mark Questions

1. Which of the following sports is not included in the Olympics?
(a) Tennis
(b) Hockey
(c) Boat Race
(d) Squash

2. How many total players are there in a team of Kabaddi?
(a) 6 (b) 7
(c) 8 (d) 5

3. Who was the first cricketer to hit a double century?
(a) Rohit Sharma
(b) Adam Gilchrist
(c) Sachin Tendulkar
(d) Virat Kohli

4. Durand Cup is related to which sport?
(a) Cricket
(b) Football
(c) Kabaddi
(d) Hockey

5. Refer to the image given below and identify the sport.

(a) Brawling (b) Fencing
(c) Judo (d) Wrestling

6. Who among the following was first time qualified for fencing in the Olympics from India?
(a) Jagmeet Kaur (b) Karan Singh
(c) Bhavani Devi (d) Josna Christy

7. Identify the sportsperson shown in the image, who won the gold medal at Commonwealth Games.

(a) Lakshya Sen (b) Prithvi Shaw
(c) Srikanth (d) Vaibhav Tomar

8. Choose the incorrectly matched pair.

Players	Sport
(a) Saina Nehwal	– Badminton
(b) Harmanpreet Kaur	– Cricket
(c) Rani Rampal	– Hockey
(d) Manu Bhaker	– Squash

9. The term 'Googly' is associated with ....

(a) hockey (b) badminton
(c) cricket (d) football

10. S Kidambi is related to which of the following sports?

(a) Chess (b) Badminton
(c) Boxing (d) Shooting

11. Commonwealth Games are held after every .... years.

(a) 4 (b) 3
(c) 6 (d) 5

12. When is National Sports Day celebrated in India?

(a) 29th August (b) 1st June
(c) 28th March (d) 15th November

13. National Sports Day commemorates the birth anniversary of ....

(a) Jawaharlal Nehru
(b) Lal Bahadur Shastri
(c) Major Dhyan Chand
(d) Kapil Dev

14. Who among the following won the first individual gold medal at the Olympics for India?

(a) Abhinav Bindra
(b) Vishwanathan Anand
(c) Neeraj Chopra
(d) Major Dhyan Chand

15. Neeraj Chopra is related to which of the following sports?

(a) Javelin Throw (b) Boxing
(c) Wrestling (d) Shooting

16. Who is the first Indian badminton player to win an Olympic Medal?

(a) Srikanth Kidambi
(b) PV Sindhu
(c) PV Nehwal
(d) Saina Nehwal

17. Complete the given analogy.

Cricket : Umpire : : Hockey : ?

(a) Goalie (b) Referee
(c) Lineperson (d) Umpire

18. BCCI is related to which of the following sports?

(a) Hockey (b) Cricket
(c) State Sports (d) Football

MCQs 2 Marks Questions

19. Read the following statements regarding the sports in India and choose the correct option.

I. Cricket is the national game of India.
II. India has won a medal in fencing in the year 2022.

Codes

(a) I and II
(b) II and III
(c) I and III
(d) None of the above

20. Read the following statements regarding boxing and identifies which ones are true (T) and which ones are false (F).

I. Bajrang Punia is related to boxing.
II. The sport of boxing is governed by the Boxing Federation of India.
III. The first Indian boxer to win an Olympic medal is Vijender Singh.

Codes

	I	II	III
(a)	T	T	T
(b)	F	F	F
(c)	F	T	T
(d)	T	F	F

21. Match the following.

	List I (Sportsperson)		**List II** (Sport)
A.	Lovlina Borgohain	1.	Boxing
B.	Sakshi Malik	2.	Wrestling
C.	Manika Batra	3.	Table Tennis
D.	PV Sindhu	4.	Badminton

Codes

	A	B	C	D		A	B	C	D
(a)	1	2	3	4	(b)	2	1	3	4
(c)	4	3	2	1	(d)	3	4	1	2

22. There are two statements marked as Assertion (A) and Reason (R). Mark your answer as per the codes given below.

Assertion (A) Khelo India is organised by the Ministry of Youth Affairs and Sports.

Reason (R) It is to promote sports culture in India.

Codes

(a) Both A and R are true and R is the correct explanation of A

(b) Both A and R are true, but R is not the correct explanation of A

(c) A is true, but R is false

(d) A is false, but R is true

23. Read the following statements regarding Hockey in India and choose the correct option.

I. Current captain of the Indian male hockey team is Manpreet Singh.

II. The captain of the female hockey team is Savita Punia.

III. The World Cup of male hockey is being held in India.

Codes

(a) I and II

(b) II and III

(c) I and III

(d) All of the above

24. Read the following statements and choose the correct option.

I. Major Dhyan Chand is known as the Wizard of Hockey.

II. The Khel Ratna Award is named after him.

Codes

(a) Only I

(b) Only II

(c) Both I and II

(d) None of the above

25. Identify the sportsperson from the description given below.

- She has won several medals at World Events for India.
- She hails from state of Manipur.

(a) Mary Kom

(b) Sakshi Malik

(c) Manu Bhaker

(d) Geeta Phogat

Darken your choice with HB Pencil

1.	ⓐ ⓑ ⓒ ⓓ	6.	ⓐ ⓑ ⓒ ⓓ	11.	ⓐ ⓑ ⓒ ⓓ	16.	ⓐ ⓑ ⓒ ⓓ	21.	ⓐ ⓑ ⓒ ⓓ
2.	ⓐ ⓑ ⓒ ⓓ	7.	ⓐ ⓑ ⓒ ⓓ	12.	ⓐ ⓑ ⓒ ⓓ	17.	ⓐ ⓑ ⓒ ⓓ	22.	ⓐ ⓑ ⓒ ⓓ
3.	ⓐ ⓑ ⓒ ⓓ	8.	ⓐ ⓑ ⓒ ⓓ	13.	ⓐ ⓑ ⓒ ⓓ	18.	ⓐ ⓑ ⓒ ⓓ	23.	ⓐ ⓑ ⓒ ⓓ
4.	ⓐ ⓑ ⓒ ⓓ	9.	ⓐ ⓑ ⓒ ⓓ	14.	ⓐ ⓑ ⓒ ⓓ	19.	ⓐ ⓑ ⓒ ⓓ	24.	ⓐ ⓑ ⓒ ⓓ
5.	ⓐ ⓑ ⓒ ⓓ	10.	ⓐ ⓑ ⓒ ⓓ	15.	ⓐ ⓑ ⓒ ⓓ	20.	ⓐ ⓑ ⓒ ⓓ	25.	ⓐ ⓑ ⓒ ⓓ

Chapter 26

Awards, Honours and Recognitions

MCQs 1 Mark Questions

1. Which of the following countries awards the prestigious Nobel Awards?
(a) United Kingdom
(b) Sweden
(c) Spain
(d) Italy

2. Who among the following was not the first recipient of Bharat Ratna Award?
(a) Jawaharlal Nehru
(b) Dr Sarvepalli Radhakrishnan
(c) CV Raman
(d) Chakravarti Rajagopalachari

3. Which of the following awards is often called as the 'Nobel Peace Prize of Asia'?
(a) Gandhi Peace Prize
(b) Ramon Magsaysay Award
(c) Sahitya Akademi Award
(d) Jnanpith Award

4. When was the first time the Nobel Prize were awarded?
(a) 1901 (b) 1969
(c) 1991 (d) 1906

5. Alfred Nobel on whose name the famous Nobel Prize has been instituted was the inventor of which of the following?
(a) Generator
(b) Dynamite
(c) Nuclear bomb
(d) Lead battery

6. Who among the following was the first Indian and also the first Asian to be awarded with Nobel Prize?
(a) CV Raman
(b) Mother Teresa
(c) Rabindranath Tagore
(d) Mahatma Gandhi

7. Which of the following awards is not given in the field of music?
(a) Saraswati Samman
(b) Grammy Awards
(c) Sangeet Natak Akademi Awards
(d) Lata Mangeshkar Award

8. Who was the first Indian recipient of the Oscar Awards?
(a) Ravi Shankar (b) Bhanu Athaiya
(c) AR Rahman (d) Gulzar

9. Ramon Magsaysay Award has been named after the former President of which of the following countries?
(a) Malaysia
(b) Vietnam
(c) Indonesia
(d) Phillipines

10. Major Dhyan Chand Khel Ratna Award was previously known by which of the following names?
(a) Milkha Singh Khel Ratna Award
(b) Mahatma Gandhi Khel Ratna Award
(c) Rajiv Gandhi Khel Ratna Award
(d) Arjuna Khel Ratna Award

11. Who among the following was the first recipient of the Rajiv Gandhi Khel Ratna Award (Major Dhyan Chand Khel Ratna Award)?
(a) Vishwanathan Anand
(b) Karnam Malleswari
(c) Abhinav Bindra
(d) Geet Sethi

12. Complete the given analogy.
Booker Prize : Literature : : Pulitzer Prize : ?
(a) Science (b) Music
(c) Journalism (d) Agriculture

13. Identify the person from the given image, who was the first non-Indian to receive the Bharat Ratna Award.

(a) Zubin Mehta
(b) Nelson Mandela
(c) Khan Abdul Gaffar khan
(d) MG Ramachandran

14. Which of the following organisations gives the Kalinga Prize in the field of Science?
(a) UNESCO (b) CSIR
(c) NBRI (d) IISC

15. Sharad Joshi on whose name an award is given is associated with which of the following?
(a) Cartoon (b) Social service
(c) Music (d) Satire and essays

16. What is the full form of BAFTA , an award given in the field of films?
(a) Bombay Awards for Film, Television and Acting
(b) Boston Academy of Films, Telefilms and Acting
(c) British Awards for Films, Television and Acting
(d) British Academy of Film and Television Arts

17. Which of the following awards is also known by the name of Academy Awards?
(a) Cannes Award (b) Oscar Award
(c) Grammy Award (d) National Film Award

18. .... is the second highest Civilian Award in India.
(a) Ashoka Chakra
(b) Param Vir Chakra
(c) Padma Vibhushan
(d) Shaurya Chakra

19. Rabindranath Tagore receive Nobel Prize in 1913 in the field of ....
(a) Physics (b) Peace
(c) Literature (d) Economy

20. Saraswati Samman is awarded by ....
(a) KK Birla Foundation
(b) Government of India
(c) Salrity Academy
(d) None of the above

21. Pulitzer price is awarded for outstanding work in the field of ....

(a) Science and Technology
(b) Environmental Studies
(c) Literature and Journalism
(d) None of the above

MCQs 2 Mark Questions

22. Which of the following statements is not true with respect to the Dadasaheb Phalke Awards?

I. It is the India's highest award in the field of cinema.

II. Dada Saheb Phalke is regarded as the Father of the Indian Cinema.

III. The first winner of this award was Prithvi Raj Kapoor.

IV. Dada Saheb Phalke directed the India's first full length feature film, Raja Harishchandra.

Codes

(a) Only I (b) I and II
(c) Only III (d) I and IV

23. Read the following statements and choose the correct option.

I. Ashoka Chakra is awarded for acts of gallantry in the presence of enemy.

II. Ashoka Chakra appears on edicts of Ashoka, most notable on Lion Capital of Ashoka.

Codes

(a) Only I
(b) Only II
(c) Both I and II
(d) None of the above

24. There are two statements marked as Assertion (A) and Reason (R). Mark your answer as per the codes given below.

Assertion (A) Highest Civilian Award of India is Bharat Ratna.

Reason (R) Highest Civilian Award is awarded to only two foreigners so far.

Codes

(a) Both A and R are true and R is the correct explanation of A
(b) Both A and R are true, but R is not the correct explanation of A
(c) A is true, but R is false
(d) A is false, but R is true

25. Read the following statements and choose the correct option.

I. The only Indian to win the Nobel Prize in physics is Dr CV Raman.

II. CV Raman and JC Bose both were awarded the Nobel Prize in physics.

Codes

(a) Only I
(b) Only II
(c) Both I and II
(d) None of the above

Darken your choice with HB Pencil

1.	ⓐ ⓑ ⓒ ⓓ	6.	ⓐ ⓑ ⓒ ⓓ	11.	ⓐ ⓑ ⓒ ⓓ	16.	ⓐ ⓑ ⓒ ⓓ	21.	ⓐ ⓑ ⓒ ⓓ
2.	ⓐ ⓑ ⓒ ⓓ	7.	ⓐ ⓑ ⓒ ⓓ	12.	ⓐ ⓑ ⓒ ⓓ	17.	ⓐ ⓑ ⓒ ⓓ	22.	ⓐ ⓑ ⓒ ⓓ
3.	ⓐ ⓑ ⓒ ⓓ	8.	ⓐ ⓑ ⓒ ⓓ	13.	ⓐ ⓑ ⓒ ⓓ	18.	ⓐ ⓑ ⓒ ⓓ	23.	ⓐ ⓑ ⓒ ⓓ
4.	ⓐ ⓑ ⓒ ⓓ	9.	ⓐ ⓑ ⓒ ⓓ	14.	ⓐ ⓑ ⓒ ⓓ	19.	ⓐ ⓑ ⓒ ⓓ	24.	ⓐ ⓑ ⓒ ⓓ
5.	ⓐ ⓑ ⓒ ⓓ	10.	ⓐ ⓑ ⓒ ⓓ	15.	ⓐ ⓑ ⓒ ⓓ	20.	ⓐ ⓑ ⓒ ⓓ	25.	ⓐ ⓑ ⓒ ⓓ

Chapter 27

General Science

MCQs 1 Mark Questions

1. Identify the metal which occupy the central position in a chlorophyll molecule.
(a) Iron (b) Copper
(c) Magnesium (d) Strontium

2. Which of the following gases is usually filled in an electric bulb?
(a) Oxygen (b) Argon
(c) Hydrogen (d) Helium

3. Identify the main constituent in the Plaster of Paris which is used for casting molds?
(a) Mica (b) Calcium carbonate
(c) Gypsum (d) Both (a) and (c)

4. Which of the following varieties of coal has the highest moisture content?
(a) Lignite (b) Peat
(c) Bituminous (d) Anthracite

5. Choose the correct statements is/are true with respect to graphite.
(a) It is used in making pencil .
(b) It is a compound of sulphur.
(c) It can be used as a lubricant.
(d) Both (a) and (c)

6. Complete the given analogy.
Solar cell : Solar energy into mechanical energy : : ? : Mechanical energy into electrical energy.
(a) Tubelight
(b) Sitar
(c) Microphone
(d) Dynamo

7. Which of the following is not an electromagnetic wave?
(a) Ultrasonic waves
(b) X-rays
(c) Radio waves
(d) Ultraviolet rays

8. Complete the given analogy.
Newton : Gravity : : Doppler : ?
(a) Heat (b) Sound
(c) Light (d) Radioactivity

9. What is the name of the gas that is mixed with LPG to provide it odour, in order to detect leakage?
(a) Methyl mercaptan
(b) Ethyl acetate
(c) Methyl isocyanate
(d) Ethyl mercaptan

10. Non-stick cooking utensils are being used by a large number of urban consumers. They are coated with which of the following?
(a) Black paint (b) Polystyrene
(c) Polysilicon (d) Teflon

11. Which of the following gases induce laughing and thus is named as laughing gas?
(a) Nitrogen dioxide (b) Sulphur dioxide
(c) Nitrous oxide (d) Nitric oxide

12. Which of the following metals remains liquid under normal conditions and is used in traditional thermometers?
(a) Uranium (b) Mercury
(c) Lead (d) Barium

13. Complete the given analogy.
Myopia : Short sightedness : : ? : Long sightedness
(a) Presbyopia
(b) Dystopia
(c) Hypermetropia
(d) Astigmatism

14. Which of the following statements is true with respect to light?
(a) It behaves as a particle.
(b) It behaves as a wave.
(c) It behaves as both particle and wave.
(d) None of the above

15. An oiled paper is an example of which of the following types of material?
(a) Opaque
(b) Transparent
(c) Translucent
(d) Both (‸) and (c)

16. Which of the following is a protein that increases the rate of chemical reaction ?
(a) Catalyst (b) Enzyme
(c) Insulin (d) Antibodies

17. Which of the following scientists is known as the father of the periodic table?
(a) Antoine Lavoisier
(b) Eugen Goldstein
(c) Dmitri Mendeleev
(d) John Newlands

18. What is meant by the term 'Apiculture'?
(a) Breeding of wasps
(b) Production of hybridised seeds
(c) Rearing of honeybee
(d) Culture of sugar loving bacteria

19. Which of the following rightly describes the dry ice?
(a) Solid carbon dioxide
(b) Supercooled water
(c) Ice at polar regions
(d) Gelatinous ice

20. Which of the following compounds is also known as the washing soda?
(a) Sodium benzoate
(b) Calcium sulphate
(c) Calcium carbonate
(d) Sodium carbonate

MCQs 2 Marks Questions

21. Consider the following statements and choose the correct option.
I. Vacuoles is present in plant cell, but absent in animal cell.
II. Cell wall is present in both animal and plant cell.

Codes
(a) Only I
(b) Only II
(c) Both I and II
(d) None of the above

22. There are two statements marked as Assertion (A) and Reason (R). Mark your answer as per the codes given below.

Assertion (A) Virus is a connecting link between living and non-living.

Reason (R) Virus has characters of both living and non-living.

Codes

(a) Both A and R are true and R is the correct explanation of A
(b) Both A and R are true, but R is not the correct explanation of A
(c) A is true, but R is false
(d) A is false, but R is true

23. Which of the following is/are the biotic components of an ecosystem?

I. Consumers
II. Climate
III. Fungi
IV. Water

Codes

(a) I, II and III
(b) II and III
(c) Only I
(d) I and III

24. Read the following statements and identifies which ones are true (T) and which ones are false (F).

I. Loss of electron results in positive charge on the element.
II. The nuclear particle having no mass and no charge, but only spin is called neutron.
III. Loss of electron makes an element an anion.

Codes

	I	II	III		I	II	III
(a)	T	T	F	(b)	T	F	T
(c)	F	T	F	(d)	F	T	T

25. Match the following.

	List I (Disease)	**List II** (Affected Organ)
A.	Meningitis	1. Immune system
B.	Trachoma	2. Brain
C.	Hepatitis	3. Eyes
D.	AIDS	4. Liver

Codes

	A	B	C	D
(a)	3	4	1	2
(b)	3	1	4	2
(c)	2	3	4	1
(d)	3	2	4	1

Darken your choice with HB Pencil

1.	ⓐ ⓑ ⓒ ⓓ	6.	ⓐ ⓑ ⓒ ⓓ	11.	ⓐ ⓑ ⓒ ⓓ	16.	ⓐ ⓑ ⓒ ⓓ	21.	ⓐ ⓑ ⓒ ⓓ
2.	ⓐ ⓑ ⓒ ⓓ	7.	ⓐ ⓑ ⓒ ⓓ	12.	ⓐ ⓑ ⓒ ⓓ	17.	ⓐ ⓑ ⓒ ⓓ	22.	ⓐ ⓑ ⓒ ⓓ
3.	ⓐ ⓑ ⓒ ⓓ	8.	ⓐ ⓑ ⓒ ⓓ	13.	ⓐ ⓑ ⓒ ⓓ	18.	ⓐ ⓑ ⓒ ⓓ	23.	ⓐ ⓑ ⓒ ⓓ
4.	ⓐ ⓑ ⓒ ⓓ	9.	ⓐ ⓑ ⓒ ⓓ	14.	ⓐ ⓑ ⓒ ⓓ	19.	ⓐ ⓑ ⓒ ⓓ	24.	ⓐ ⓑ ⓒ ⓓ
5.	ⓐ ⓑ ⓒ ⓓ	10.	ⓐ ⓑ ⓒ ⓓ	15.	ⓐ ⓑ ⓒ ⓓ	20.	ⓐ ⓑ ⓒ ⓓ	25.	ⓐ ⓑ ⓒ ⓓ

Chapter 28

General Awareness

(Books & Authors, Research Institutions, Abbreviations, Capital & Currencies, International Organisations)

MCQs 1 Mark Questions

1. The primary scripture of Sikhism the Guru Granth Sahib is written in Gurmukhi script. Who among the following invented this script?

(a) Guru Nanak
(b) Guru Angad
(c) Guru Gobind Singh
(d) Guru Tegh Bahadur

2. Which of the following books is authored by Chetan Bhagat?

(a) 3 Mistakes of My Life
(b) The Immortals of Meluha
(c) Your Dreams are Mine Now
(d) Life is What You Make it

3. Which of the following is not true with respect to Dadabhai Naoroji?

(a) He was also known as the 'Grand Old Man of India'.
(b) He gave the drain of wealth theory.
(c) He was a Parsi.
(d) He was an extremist leader.

4. Who among the following took 25 years to complete the famous novel 'A Suitable Boy'?

(a) Devdutt Pattanaik
(b) Shashi Tharoor
(c) Vikram Seth
(d) Durjoy Datta

5. Which of the following statements is not true with respect to the writer of the famous book 'Gitanjali'?

(a) He was the 2nd Asian to win Nobel Prize in literature.
(b) He was the 1st Indian to win Nobel Prize in literature.
(c) He also wrote the book 'Kabuliwala'.
(d) He set up Shantiniketan.

6. Our national song is written in which of the following novels?

(a) Devi Chaudhurani
(b) Devdas
(c) Anandamath
(d) Nirmala

7. CDRI is one of the premier research institute. It is dedicated to the research in which of the following fields?
(a) Dermatology (b) Drugs
(c) Detergents (d) Demography

8. Central Rice Research Institute located in Cuttack develops new rice varieties and rice crop management techniques. Which of the following statements is not true with regard to rice crop?
(a) Rice crop requires lots of water.
(b) Rice crop requires hot and humid climate.
(c) Rice is best grown on laterite soil.
(d) Rice is a kharif crop.

9. Karnal, the headquarters of the National Dairy Research Institute is situated in which of the following states?
(a) Punjab
(b) Himachal Pradesh
(c) Rajasthan
(d) Haryana

10. Netaji Subhash National Institute of Sports, the Asia's largest sport institute is located at which of the following places?
(a) Delhi (b) Jalandhar
(c) Patiala (d) Mohali

11. Which of the following is statements true with respect to the ISRO?
(a) It is the national space agency of Bangladesh.
(b) It is headquartered in Chennai.
(c) It was founded in 1968.
(d) It's founder was Vikram Sarabhai.

12. ASEAN is an important association of ten nation states. What is the correct full form of ASEAN?
(a) Association of Southern Economic Asian Nations
(b) Association of South East Asian Nations
(c) Association of Sea Entrance Asian Nations
(d) Association of Super Economically Active Nations

13. Complete the given anology.
IMF : International Monetary Fund : : ADB : ?
(a) Asian Development Bank
(b) African Debt Bank
(c) American Development Bank
(d) None of the above

14. BBC, a news agency based in London stands for ....
(a) British Broadcasting Company
(b) Broadcasting Business Company
(c) Britain Broadcasting Centre
(d) British Broadcasting Corporation

15. BRICS, an association of five nations consists of which of the following countries?
(a) Britain, Russia, Indonesia, Canada , Sweden
(b) Brazil, Russia, India, Canada, South Africa
(c) Brazil, Russia , India, China, South Africa
(d) Brazil, Russia, India, China, Sri Lanka

16. In the context of international environmental efforts , what does the term 'REDD' stand for?
(a) Reduction in Environmental Degradation and Desertification
(b) Reduce Environmental Damage and Degradation
(c) Reducing Emissions from Deforestation and Forest Degradation
(d) Reducing Emissions from Developmental and Degradations

17. Which of the following capital cities of India is known by the ancient name of Patliputra?

(a) Lucknow (b) Panaji
(c) Ranchi (d) Patna

18. Which of the following cities is not the capital city of an Asian country?

(a) Phnom Penh (b) Rio de Janeiro
(c) Baku (d) Manila

19. Complete the given analogy.

USA : Dollar : : Argentina : ?

(a) Euro (b) Rial
(c) Paisa (d) Peso

20. The world's strongest currency belongs to which of the following countries?

(a) America (b) Kuwait
(c) Iran (d) Britain

21. The objective of which of the following organisations is to ensure the optimal use of the world's resources by establishing a rule based trading system and is headquartered in Geneva?

(a) WTO (b) UNIDO
(c) IMF (d) OECD

22. Which of the following is not a G-20 country?

(a) China (b) India
(c) Mexico (d) Chile

23. Which of the following is the parent organisation of World Health Organisation?

(a) United Nations
(b) UNICEF
(c) European Union
(d) ASEAN

24. Which of the following countries is not a permanent member of UNSC?

(a) USA (b) Soviet union
(c) Germany (d) France

25. Bretton Woods Agreement led to the formation of which of the following institutions?

(a) International Monetary Fund
(b) World Bank
(c) Both (a) and (b)
(d) United Nations

MCQs 2 Marks Questions

26. Identify the famous personality with the help of the following information.

He is called as father of nuclear physics in India and is the founding director of the Tata Institute of Fundamental Research.

(a) Homi J Bhabha (b) Vikram Sarabhai
(c) CV Raman (d) JC Bose

27. Which of the following novels are written by Munshi Premchand?

I. Gaban II. Godan
III. Nirmala IV. Gunaho ka Devta

Codes

(a) II and III (b) II, III and IV
(c) I, II and III (d) I, II and IV

28. Match the following.

List I (Research Institutes)	List II (Headquarters)
A. Indian Veterinary Research Institute	1. New Delhi
B. Indian Agriculture Research Institute	2. Thiruvananthap-uram
C. National Environmental Engineering Research Institute	3. Bareilly
D. Vikram Sarabhai Space Centre	4. Nagpur

Codes

	A	B	C	D		A	B	C	D
(a)	4	3	1	2	(b)	3	1	4	2
(c)	3	2	1	4	(d)	1	2	3	4

29. Which of the following full forms are correct?

I. GDP – Gross Development Product

II. ILO – Indian Labour Organisation

III. AIDS – Acquired Immuno Deficiency Syndrome

Codes

(a) II and III (b) I, II and III

(c) I and III (d) II and I

30. Match the following.

List I (Countries)	**List II** (Currencies)
A. China	1. Renminbi
B. Bangladesh	2. Rand
C. Iran	3. Taka
D. South Africa	4. Rial

Codes

	A	B	C	D
(a)	1	4	2	3
(b)	4	3	2	1
(c)	1	3	4	2
(d)	1	3	2	4

31. Read the following statements and choose the correct option.

I. The book Kadambari was written by Banabhatta.

II. The book Meghaduta was written by Kalidasa.

III. Colombo is the Capital city of Sri Lanka.

Codes

(a) Only I

(b) Only II

(c) I and III

(d) I, II and III

Darken your choice with HB Pencil

1. ⓐ ⓑ ⓒ ⓓ	7. ⓐ ⓑ ⓒ ⓓ	13. ⓐ ⓑ ⓒ ⓓ	19. ⓐ ⓑ ⓒ ⓓ	25. ⓐ ⓑ ⓒ ⓓ	31. ⓐ ⓑ ⓒ ⓓ
2. ⓐ ⓑ ⓒ ⓓ	8. ⓐ ⓑ ⓒ ⓓ	14. ⓐ ⓑ ⓒ ⓓ	20. ⓐ ⓑ ⓒ ⓓ	26. ⓐ ⓑ ⓒ ⓓ	
3. ⓐ ⓑ ⓒ ⓓ	9. ⓐ ⓑ ⓒ ⓓ	15. ⓐ ⓑ ⓒ ⓓ	21. ⓐ ⓑ ⓒ ⓓ	27. ⓐ ⓑ ⓒ ⓓ	
4. ⓐ ⓑ ⓒ ⓓ	10. ⓐ ⓑ ⓒ ⓓ	16. ⓐ ⓑ ⓒ ⓓ	22. ⓐ ⓑ ⓒ ⓓ	28. ⓐ ⓑ ⓒ ⓓ	
5. ⓐ ⓑ ⓒ ⓓ	11. ⓐ ⓑ ⓒ ⓓ	17. ⓐ ⓑ ⓒ ⓓ	23. ⓐ ⓑ ⓒ ⓓ	29. ⓐ ⓑ ⓒ ⓓ	
6. ⓐ ⓑ ⓒ ⓓ	12. ⓐ ⓑ ⓒ ⓓ	18. ⓐ ⓑ ⓒ ⓓ	24. ⓐ ⓑ ⓒ ⓓ	30. ⓐ ⓑ ⓒ ⓓ	

Practice Set 01

Time : 60 Mins. Max. Marks : 60

General Instructions

1. This question paper contains 50 questions.
2. All questions are compulsory. There is no negative marking.
3. Q. No. 1 to 40 are of 1 mark each and Q. No. 41 to 50 are of 2 marks each.
4. Use HB pencil / Blue ball point pen to mark your choice of answer by darkening the circles on the OMR Sheet.

MCQs 1 Mark Questions

1. Under whose reign the Chinese traveller Fa-hein came to India?
(a) Samudragupta
(b) Kumaragupta
(c) Skandagupta
(d) Chandragupta II

2. Which of the following was the successor of Qutb-ud-Din Aibak?
(a) Aramshah
(b) Iltutmish
(c) Ruknuddin Firuz Shah
(d) Razia Sultan

3. Which of the following Govrnal Generals of India introduced the Permanent Settlement?
(a) Thomas Munro
(b) Cornwallis
(c) Holt Mackenzie
(d) Robert Clive

4. Identify the name of the personality who is also known as 'The Grand Old Man of India'.
(a) Lala Lajpat Rai
(b) Dadabhai Naoroji
(c) Bal Gangadhar Tilak
(d) Bipin Chandra Pal

5. The Second World War began in which of the following years?
(a) 1910 (b) 1914 (c) 1939 (d) 1920

6. Identify the classical dance form which is shown in the image given below.

(a) Kathakali (b) Kuchipudi
(c) Odissi (d) Bharatnatyam

7. Complete the given analogy.
Ramayana : Valmiki :: Abhijnana Shakuntalam : ?
(a) Vyasa (b) Kalidasa
(c) Charaka (d) Vishvamitra

8. Identify the planets which are known as the 'Jovian Planets'.
(a) Jupiter, Saturn, Uranus, Neptune
(b) Mars, Jupiter, Saturn, Uranus
(c) Saturn, Uranus, Neptune, Pluto
(d) Mercury, Venus, Earth, Mars

9. Which of the following celestial phenomena occurs due to stars?
(a) Ozone (b) Black hole
(c) Rainbow (d) Comet

10. Which of the following places receive the highest rainfall in India?
(a) Mawsynram (b) Cherrapunji
(c) Mahabaleshwar (d) Pasighat

11. Name the language that is widely spoken by the people residing in Kerala.
(a) Hindi (b) Konkani
(c) Oriya (d) Malayalam

12. Complete the given analogy.
Bandhavgarh National Park : Madhya Pradesh :: Dudhwa National Park : ?
(a) Uttar Pradesh (b) Rajasthan
(c) Odisha (d) Maharashtra

13. The main cause of global climatic change is …………
(a) increase in the content of carbon dioxide in the atmosphere
(b) emissions of industrial gases
(c) adding of dust
(d) changes in plant cover

14. Monsoon is caused by ……… .
(a) revolution of Earth
(b) movement of clouds
(c) seasonal reversal of winds
(d) rise in temperature

15. Identify the name of the most populous Continent in the world with the help of the image given below.

(a) Asia (b) Africa
(c) South America (d) Australia

16. Identify the correctly matched pair.

Mountains	States
(a) Vindhya Range	– Uttarakhand
(b) Cardamom Hills	– Odisha
(c) Aravalli Range	– Telangana
(d) Zaskar Range	– Kashmir

17. Identify the name of the interconnection given below.

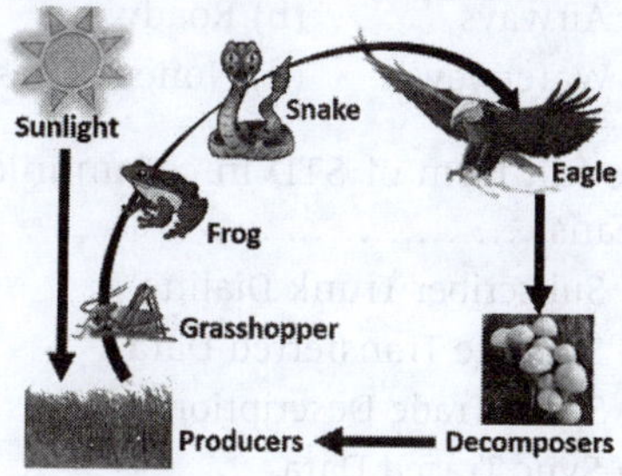

(a) Food chain
(b) Food web
(c) Food survival
(d) Ecological food connection

18. What is the value of all final goods and services produced within a country during a particular year called?
(a) Net Domestic Product
(b) Gross Domestic Product
(c) National product
(d) Production of Tertiory sector

19. Complete the given analogy.
Mining and Quarrying : Primary sector activity :: Commerce and Administration : ?
(a) Primary sector activity
(b) Secondary sector activity
(c) Tertiary sector activity
(d) None of the above

20. The term 'Sericulture' is related to…………………….. .
(a) agriculture
(b) rearing silkworms
(c) cultivation of cotton
(d) breeding of fish

21. Which of the following is the largest industry of India?
(a) Textile Industry
(b) Automobile Industry
(c) Chemical and Fertiliser
(d) Pharmaceutical

22. .... is the cheapest mode of transportation.
(a) Airways (b) Roadways
(c) Waterways (d) None of these

23. The full form of STD in communication means ....
(a) Subscriber Trunk Dialing
(b) Satellite Transferred Data
(c) Spam Trade Description
(d) Sync Traced Data

24. Identify the name of the state which has the highest literacy rate in India as per census 2011.
(a) Madhya Pradesh
(b) Chhattisgarh
(c) Kerala
(d) Jharkhand

25. Complete the given analogy.
Russia : Ruble : : Japan : ?
(a) Ruble (b) Yen
(c) Pound (d) Euro

26. The original Constitution of India was hand written by ....
(a) Prem Behari Narain Raizada
(b) Dr BR Ambedkar
(c) Lal Bahadur Shastri
(d) Rajendra Prasad

27. Constitution Day is celebrated in our country on ....
(a) 24th November
(b) 25th November
(c) 26th November
(d) 27th November

28. The Fundamental Duties are explained in which part of the Constitution?
(a) Part–IV A (b) Part – II
(c) Part–III A (d) Part – IV

29. Which of the following is also known as the 'Magna Carta' of Indian Constitution?
(a) Directive Principles of State Policies
(b) Fundamental Duties
(c) Fundamental Rights
(d) Citizenship

30. In India, at the state level, the executive comprises the Chief Minister, Council of Ministers and the ....
(a) President (b) Prime Minister
(c) Chief Justice (d) Governor

31. What is the full form of PESA?
(a) The Provisions of the Panchayats Extension to the Scheduled Areas
(b) Panchayat and Executive System of Administration
(c) Panchayat Extended in Scheduled Administrations
(d) Panchayat Emerged to Scheduled Areas

32. Identify the name of the personality who is known as the Father of the Panchayati Raj in India with the help of the image given below.

(a) Balwant Rai Mehta
(b) Rajeev Gandhi
(c) Ashok Mehta
(d) P K Thungon

33. ISRO related to which of the following terms?

(a) Defence and Security
(b) Flora and Fauna
(c) Space and Technology
(d) Robotics

34. Identify the type of plant with the help of the image given below.

(a) Autotrophes
(b) Insectivorous
(c) Saprophytes
(d) None of the above

35. The first recipient of Rajiv Gandhi's 'Khel Ratna' Award is

(a) Viswanathan Anand
(b) Leander Peas
(c) Yuvraj Singh
(d) Milkha Singh

36. The terms French Open, Wimbledon and Australian Open are associated with ....

(a) Badminton
(b) Tennis
(c) Table Tennis
(d) Hockey

37. Which among the following awards is given in the field of Medical Science?

(a) Juliet Curie Award
(b) Dhyanwantari
(c) Pampa Award
(d) Awadh Samman

38. Which is the highest literary award of the world?

(a) Booker Prize
(b) Pulitzer Prize
(c) Nobel Prize
(d) Magsaysay Award

39. Canberra is the capital city of ....

(a) Argentina
(b) Sudan
(c) Australia
(d) Brazil

40. Which of the following leaders has authored the book 'Hind Swaraj'?

(a) Bhagat Singh
(b) Mahatma Gandhi
(c) Chandra Shekhar Azad
(d) Bal Gangadhar Tilak

MCQs 2 Marks Questions

41. Which of the following are the challenge faced by Panchayati Raj in India?

I. lack of finances
II. Administrative problem
III. Political interference
IV. Over population

Codes

(a) I, II and III
(b) II and IV
(c) II and IV
(d) All of the above

42. Identify the name of the Nobel winner with the help of the information given below.

- He is an Indian social reformer who campaigned against the child labour in India.
- He also initiated the 'Bachpan Bachao Andolan'.

(a) Satyajit Ray (b) Kailash Satyarthi
(c) Bhanu Athaiya (d) None of these

43. Read the following statements and choose the correct option.

I. The Governor appoint the Chief Minister of a State.

II. The Governor of a State is appointed by the Prime Minister.

III. The Chief Minister is an elected head of the State.

Codes

(a) I and II

(b) I and III

(c) II and III

(d) All of the above

44. Match the following.

List I (Diseases)		List II (Affected organ)
A. Rickets	1.	Liver
B. Tuberculosis	2.	Heart
C. Cardiac arrest	3.	Bones
D. Jaundice	4.	Lungs

Codes

	A	B	C	D
(a)	3	4	2	1
(b)	1	3	4	2
(c)	2	1	3	4
(d)	2	3	4	1

45. Identify the name of the power generating system with the help of the information given below.

- Norway was the first country to develop this system.
- It is a renewable source of energy that generates power by using a dam or diversion structure to alter the natural flow of a river or other body of water.

(a) Nuclear power (b) Hydel power

(c) Solar power (d) Geothermal power

46. Identify the name of the crop which is leading production of the marked (A) region.

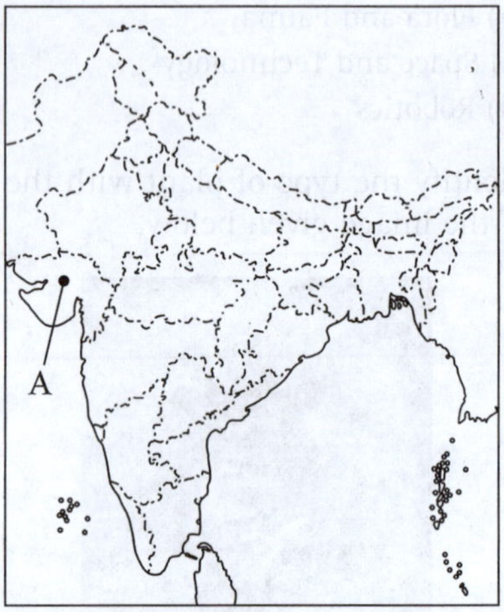

Codes

(a) Jute

(b) Cotton

(c) Wheat

(d) Sugarcane

47. There are two statements marked as Assertion (A) and Reason (R). Mark your answer as per the codes given below.

Assertion (A) Mughal Administration witnessed the downfall of the Empire after the reign of Aurangzeb.

Reason (R) Later, Mughal Emperors were incapable and inefficient rulers.

Codes

(a) Both A and R are true and R is the correct explanation of A

(b) Both A and R are true but R is not the correct explanation of A

(c) A is true but R is false

(d) A is false and R is true

48. Read the following statements and identifies which ones are true (T) and which ones are false (F).

I. Horticulture is related to the cultivation of fruits and vegetables.

II. Pesticides are used to increase the yield of the crop.

III. Sericulture is related to the maintenance of honeybees and hives.

IV. Verghese Kurien is also known as the Father of Indian Green Revolution.

Codes

	I	II	III	IV
(a)	T	T	T	F
(b)	T	F	F	F
(c)	F	T	T	F
(d)	F	T	T	T

49. Read the following statements and choose the correct option.

I. In Bhakti Movement, the Nayanars were associated with the devotion of Lord Vishnu.

II. Razia Sultan belonged to the Slave Dynasty of Delhi Sultanate.

Codes

(a) Only I (b) Only II
(c) Both I and II (d) None of these

50. Identify the national park with the help of the information given below.

- It is situated in the state of Assam.
- It is a part of the UNESCO World Heritage Site.

(a) Kaziranga National Park
(b) Sundarban National Park
(c) Kanha National Park
(d) Valmiki National Park

Darken your choice with HB Pencil

1. ⓐ ⓑ ⓒ ⓓ	10. ⓐ ⓑ ⓒ ⓓ	19. ⓐ ⓑ ⓒ ⓓ	28. ⓐ ⓑ ⓒ ⓓ	37. ⓐ ⓑ ⓒ ⓓ	46. ⓐ ⓑ ⓒ ⓓ
2. ⓐ ⓑ ⓒ ⓓ	11. ⓐ ⓑ ⓒ ⓓ	20. ⓐ ⓑ ⓒ ⓓ	29. ⓐ ⓑ ⓒ ⓓ	38. ⓐ ⓑ ⓒ ⓓ	47. ⓐ ⓑ ⓒ ⓓ
3. ⓐ ⓑ ⓒ ⓓ	12. ⓐ ⓑ ⓒ ⓓ	21. ⓐ ⓑ ⓒ ⓓ	30. ⓐ ⓑ ⓒ ⓓ	39. ⓐ ⓑ ⓒ ⓓ	48. ⓐ ⓑ ⓒ ⓓ
4. ⓐ ⓑ ⓒ ⓓ	13. ⓐ ⓑ ⓒ ⓓ	22. ⓐ ⓑ ⓒ ⓓ	31. ⓐ ⓑ ⓒ ⓓ	40. ⓐ ⓑ ⓒ ⓓ	49. ⓐ ⓑ ⓒ ⓓ
5. ⓐ ⓑ ⓒ ⓓ	14. ⓐ ⓑ ⓒ ⓓ	23. ⓐ ⓑ ⓒ ⓓ	32. ⓐ ⓑ ⓒ ⓓ	41. ⓐ ⓑ ⓒ ⓓ	50. ⓐ ⓑ ⓒ ⓓ
6. ⓐ ⓑ ⓒ ⓓ	15. ⓐ ⓑ ⓒ ⓓ	24. ⓐ ⓑ ⓒ ⓓ	33. ⓐ ⓑ ⓒ ⓓ	42. ⓐ ⓑ ⓒ ⓓ	
7. ⓐ ⓑ ⓒ ⓓ	16. ⓐ ⓑ ⓒ ⓓ	25. ⓐ ⓑ ⓒ ⓓ	34. ⓐ ⓑ ⓒ ⓓ	43. ⓐ ⓑ ⓒ ⓓ	
8. ⓐ ⓑ ⓒ ⓓ	17. ⓐ ⓑ ⓒ ⓓ	26. ⓐ ⓑ ⓒ ⓓ	35. ⓐ ⓑ ⓒ ⓓ	44. ⓐ ⓑ ⓒ ⓓ	
9. ⓐ ⓑ ⓒ ⓓ	18. ⓐ ⓑ ⓒ ⓓ	27. ⓐ ⓑ ⓒ ⓓ	36. ⓐ ⓑ ⓒ ⓓ	45. ⓐ ⓑ ⓒ ⓓ	

Practice Set 02

Time : 60 Mins. Max. Marks : 60

General Instructions

1. This question paper contains 50 questions.
2. All questions are compulsory. There is no negative marking.
3. Q. No. 1 to 40 are of 1 mark each and Q. No. 41 to 50 are of 2 marks each.
4. Use HB pencil / Blue ball point pen to mark your choice of answer by darkening the circles on the OMR Sheet.

MCQs 1 Mark Questions

1. Which of the following were the first to issue gold coins?

(a) Shakas (b) Parthians
(c) Indo-Greeks (d) Kushana

2. The rulers of Rashtrakutas belonged to the region of ....

(a) Bengal (b) Deccan
(c) Rajasthan (d) None of these

3. The first woman President of the Indian National Congress was ....

(a) Annie Besant
(b) Madam Bhikaji Cama
(c) Sarojini Naidu
(d) Rajkumari Amrit Kaur

4. The provision of Single Citizenship has been taken from which of the following Constitutions?

(a) USA
(b) Ireland
(c) United Kingdom
(d) Russia

5. Which among the following were the Axis Powers in World War II?

(a) Poland, Japan, Germany
(b) Italy, Japan, Britain
(c) Germany, Italy, France
(d) Germany, Italy, Japan

6. Identify the name of the painting which is shown in the image given below.

(a) Patachitra (b) Gond
(c) Warli (d) Madhubani

7. Complete the given analogy.

Bijak : Kabir Das:: Meghaduta : ?

(a) Vyasa (b) Kalidasa
(c) Charaka (d) Vishvamitra

8. .... are cosmic snowballs of frozen gases, rock and dust that orbit the Sun.

(a) Comet (b) Asteroid
(c) Meteor (d) Stars

9. The famous Indian Space Programme 'MOM Mission' was related to which of the following celestial bodies?

(a) Mercury (b) Mars
(c) Moon (d) None of these

10. .... is the deepest and largest ocean of the world.
(a) Indian (b) Pacific
(c) Antarctic (d) Arctic

11. The largest desert of the world 'Sahara' is located in ....
(a) Asia (b) Africa
(c) Australia (d) Europe

12. Complete the given analogy.
Sundarban National Park : West Bengal : : Ranthambore National Park : ?
(a) Uttar Pradesh (b) Rajasthan
(c) Odisha (d) Maharashtra

13. Which among the following pilgrimage sites is/are located in Himachal Himalayas?
(a) Yamunotri
(b) Kedarnath
(c) Badrinath
(d) All of the above

14. The Kharif Crops are sown in which of the following months in India?
(a) November (b) March
(c) July (d) September

15. Identify the name of the continent that is also known as the 'Black Continent' with the help of the image given below.

(a) Asia (b) Africa
(c) South America (d) Australia

16. Choose the incorrectly matched pair.

Continent	Related Countries
(a) Africa	– Kenya
(b) Asia	– Singapore
(c) Europe	– Greece
(d) North America	– Brazil

17. Which continent is situated between the Atlantic and Pacific Ocean?
(a) Africa
(b) South America
(c) Asia
(d) North America

18. .... is an important hub of Information and Technology sector in India.
(a) Bengaluru
(b) Karnataka
(c) Kerala
(d) Mumbai

19. Which of the following can be considered as an example of the economic activity extraction of minerals from the industry sector?
(a) Tourism industry
(b) Iron and Steel industry
(c) Banking industry
(d) Coal mining industry

20. Which sector has emerged as the largest producing sector in India?
(a) Primary sector
(b) Tertiary sector
(c) Secondary sector
(d) None of the above

21. .... sector industries are owned, managed and controlled by the State or Central Government.
(a) Cooperative
(b) Public
(c) Joint
(d) Private

22. Which of the following articles of the Constitution has abolished untouchability?
(a) Article 15
(b) Article 19
(c) Article 17
(d) Article 14

23. The cities of Delhi and Amritsar are connected by which of the following highways?
(a) National Highway–1
(b) National Highway–2
(c) National Highway–3
(d) National Highway–4

24. Identify the name of the state that is also known as 'The tea garden of India'.
(a) Nagaland (b) Manipur
(c) Assam (d) Mizoram

25. Complete the given analogy.
UK : Pound :: Bangladesh : ?
(a) Ruble
(b) Yen
(c) Pound
(d) Taka

26. The idea of Preamble was borrowed from which of the following countries?
(a) USA (b) Japan
(c) UK (d) Australia

27. The Constitution of India was adopted on ....
(a) 26th November, 1950
(b) 26th January, 1950
(c) 26th November, 1949
(d) 26th January, 1949

28. The 'Abolition of Untouchability' is enshrined in the Article .... of the Indian Constitution.
(a) 17 (b) 20
(c) 25 (d) 29

29. Which amendement deleted the Right to Property from Fundamental Rights?
(a) 43rd
(b) 46th
(c) 44th
(d) 42nd

30. The Indian Parliament comprises of the Lok Sabha, Rajya Sabha and the ....
(a) President
(b) Prime Minister
(c) Chief Justice
(d) Governor

31. What is the main purpose of Panchayati Raj System?
(a) To create employment
(b) To increase urbanisation
(c) To make people empowered
(d) To make people participate in developmental administration.

32. .... is an intermediate level of Panchayati system.
(a) Zila Parishad
(b) Gram Samiti
(c) Block Parishad
(d) Block Panchayat

33. .... is used to measure the purity of the milk.
(a) Ammeter
(b) Hygrometer
(c) Lactometer
(d) Thermometer

34. Complete the given analogy.
Missile Man of India : Dr Abdul Kalam : : Father of Indian Space Programme : ?
(a) CV Raman
(b) Vikram Sarabhai
(c) K. Sivan
(d) None of the above

35. The first recipient of Magsaysay Award is ....

(a) Vinoba Bhave
(b) Leander Peas
(c) TN Seshan
(d) Milkha Singh

36. Identify the name of the award related to cinema which is shown in the image given below.

(a) Dada Saheb Phalke Award
(b) Oscar Award
(c) Filmfare Award
(d) Dada Saheb Phalke Award

37. Identify the incorrectly matched pair.

Award	Category
(a) Bihari Samman	– Literature
(b) Dronacharya Award	– Sports Coach
(c) Tansen Award	– Music
(d) Kabir Samman	– Peace

38. Milk, eggs, cheese, yogurt and fish are rich source of ....

(a) carbohydrates
(b) sugar
(c) Calcium
(d) Vitamin C

39. Thimphu is the capital city of ....

(a) Bangladesh (b) Sri Lanka
(c) Bhutan (d) Nepal

40. Which of the following leaders has authored the book 'Annihilation of Castes'?

(a) Bhagat Singh
(b) Dr BR Ambedkar
(c) Chandra Shekhar Azad
(d) Bal Gangadhar Tilak

MCQs 2 Marks Questions

41. Read the following statements and choose the incorrect option.

I. The National Panchayati Raj Day is observed on 24th April.
II. The Constitution of India mandates that the elections of the Panchayati Raj should be held regularly after a gap of 3 years.

Codes

(a) Only I
(b) Only II
(c) Both I and II
(d) None of the above

42. Identify the award with the help of the information given below.

- The award was previously called as Rajiv Gandhi Khel Ratna Award.
- It is the highest sporting honour of India.

(a) Major Dhyan Chand Khel Ratna Award
(b) Dronacharya Award
(c) Rashtriya Khel Protsahan Puruskar
(d) Maulana Abul Kalam Azad Trophy

43. Read the following statements and choose the correct option.

I. The President appoint the Governor of a State.

II. The Judge of Supreme Court is appointed by the Prime Minister.

III. Prime Minister is a nominal head of the State.

Codes

(a) Only I

(b) I and III

(c) II and III

(d) I, II and III

44. Match the following.

List I (Disease)	**List II** (Deficient elements)
A. Rickets	1. Iron
B. Night Blindness	2. Calcium
C. Brittle bones	3. Vitamin D
D. Anaemia	4. Vitamin A

Codes

	A	B	C	D
(a)	3	4	2	1
(b)	1	3	4	2
(c)	2	1	3	4
(d)	2	3	4	1

45. Identify the name of the power generating system with the help of the information given below.

- It is a renewable source of energy in which animal manure, municipal rubbish or waste, plant material, food waste or sewage.
- It is a facility that provides oxygen-free conditions where anaerobic digestion can occur for reaction.

(a) Biogas power plant

(b) Hydel power

(c) Solar power

(d) Geothermal power

46. Identify the name of the crop according to the location marked as A in the map given below. It is the largest producers of this crop and industry.

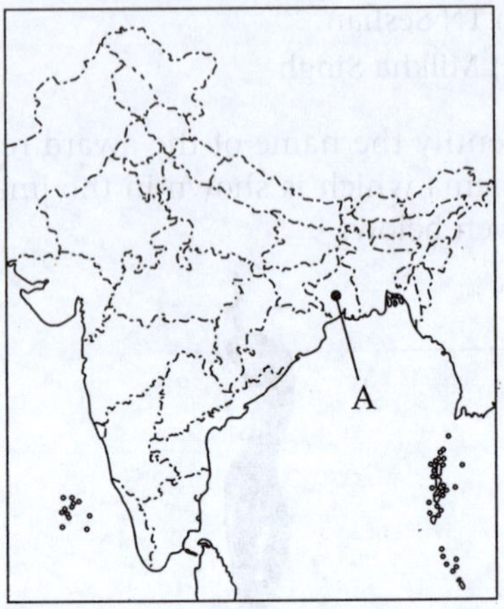

(a) Jute

(b) Cotton

(c) Wheat

(d) Sugarcane

47. There are two statements marked as Assertion (A) and Reason (R). Mark your answer as per the codes given below.

Assertion (A) Alauddin Khalji was the most efficient ruler of Delhi Sultanate.

Reason (R) He laid the foundations of Delhi Sultanate.

Codes

(a) Both A and R are true and R is the correct explanation of A

(b) Both A and R are true, but R is not the correct explanation of A

(c) A is true, but R is false

(d) A is false, but R is true

48. Read the following statements and identifies which ones are true (T) and which ones are false (F).

I. Jhum Cultivation is also known as 'slash and burn' technique.

II. HYV seeds are used to increase the yield of crops.

III. Apiculture is related to the fisheries and marine industries.

IV. MS Swaminathan is also known as the 'Milkman of India'.

Codes

	I	II	III	IV
(a)	T	T	F	F
(b)	T	F	T	T
(c)	F	T	F	F
(d)	F	F	F	F

49. Read the following statements and choose the correct option.

I. Syed Ahmad Khan was the founder of the Aligarh Muslim University.

II. Warren Hastings was the first Governor-General of Bengal.

Codes

(a) Only I

(b) Only II

(c) Both I and II

(d) None of the above

50. Identify the name of personality related to the Chipko Andolan in Uttarakhand.

- He was a famous Environmentalist.
- He fought for the preservation of forests in the Himalayas.

Codes

(a) Jadev Payeng

(b) Sunderlal Bahuguna

(c) Salim Ali

(d) Rajendra Singh

Darken your choice with HB Pencil

1.	ⓐ ⓑ ⓒ ⓓ	10.	ⓐ ⓑ ⓒ ⓓ	19.	ⓐ ⓑ ⓒ ⓓ	28.	ⓐ ⓑ ⓒ ⓓ	37.	ⓐ ⓑ ⓒ ⓓ	46.	ⓐ ⓑ ⓒ ⓓ
2.	ⓐ ⓑ ⓒ ⓓ	11.	ⓐ ⓑ ⓒ ⓓ	20.	ⓐ ⓑ ⓒ ⓓ	29.	ⓐ ⓑ ⓒ ⓓ	38.	ⓐ ⓑ ⓒ ⓓ	47.	ⓐ ⓑ ⓒ ⓓ
3.	ⓐ ⓑ ⓒ ⓓ	12.	ⓐ ⓑ ⓒ ⓓ	21.	ⓐ ⓑ ⓒ ⓓ	30.	ⓐ ⓑ ⓒ ⓓ	39.	ⓐ ⓑ ⓒ ⓓ	48.	ⓐ ⓑ ⓒ ⓓ
4.	ⓐ ⓑ ⓒ ⓓ	13.	ⓐ ⓑ ⓒ ⓓ	22.	ⓐ ⓑ ⓒ ⓓ	31.	ⓐ ⓑ ⓒ ⓓ	40.	ⓐ ⓑ ⓒ ⓓ	49.	ⓐ ⓑ ⓒ ⓓ
5.	ⓐ ⓑ ⓒ ⓓ	14.	ⓐ ⓑ ⓒ ⓓ	23.	ⓐ ⓑ ⓒ ⓓ	32.	ⓐ ⓑ ⓒ ⓓ	41.	ⓐ ⓑ ⓒ ⓓ	50.	ⓐ ⓑ ⓒ ⓓ
6.	ⓐ ⓑ ⓒ ⓓ	15.	ⓐ ⓑ ⓒ ⓓ	24.	ⓐ ⓑ ⓒ ⓓ	33.	ⓐ ⓑ ⓒ ⓓ	42.	ⓐ ⓑ ⓒ ⓓ		
7.	ⓐ ⓑ ⓒ ⓓ	16.	ⓐ ⓑ ⓒ ⓓ	25.	ⓐ ⓑ ⓒ ⓓ	34.	ⓐ ⓑ ⓒ ⓓ	43.	ⓐ ⓑ ⓒ ⓓ		
8.	ⓐ ⓑ ⓒ ⓓ	17.	ⓐ ⓑ ⓒ ⓓ	26.	ⓐ ⓑ ⓒ ⓓ	35.	ⓐ ⓑ ⓒ ⓓ	44.	ⓐ ⓑ ⓒ ⓓ		
9.	ⓐ ⓑ ⓒ ⓓ	18.	ⓐ ⓑ ⓒ ⓓ	27.	ⓐ ⓑ ⓒ ⓓ	36.	ⓐ ⓑ ⓒ ⓓ	45.	ⓐ ⓑ ⓒ ⓓ		

Answer Sheet

Chapter 01

1. (a)	2. (d)	3. (d)	4. (c)	5. (b)	6. (c)	7. (b)	8. (b)	9. (b)	10. (d)
11. (b)	12. (b)	13. (c)	14. (b)	15. (a)	16. (b)	17. (d)	18. (a)	19. (d)	20. (b)
21. (d)	22. (b)	23. (b)	24. (c)	25. (c)	26. (a)	27. (b)	28. (d)		

Chapter 02

1. (d)	2. (a)	3. (a)	4. (a)	5. (a)	6. (b)	7. (b)	8. (a)	9. (b)	10. (b)
11. (a)	12. (d)	13. (d)	14. (a)	15. (d)	16. (a)	17. (d)	18. (b)	19. (a)	20. (b)
21. (b)	22. (a)	23. (a)	24. (a)	25. (a)	26. (b)				

Chapter 03

1. (a)	2. (b)	3. (d)	4. (a)	5. (a)	6. (b)	7. (a)	8. (a)	9. (a)	10. (b)
11. (a)	12. (a)	13. (a)	14. (c)	15. (b)	16. (d)	17. (d)	18. (d)	19. (a)	20. (d)
21. (d)	22. (a)	23. (a)	24. (d)	25. (c)	26. (a)	27. (c)	28. (a)	29. (b)	30. (b)

Chapter 04

1. (c)	2. (b)	3. (d)	4. (b)	5. (d)	6. (b)	7. (a)	8. (b)	9. (d)	10. (d)
11. (b)	12. (d)	13. (a)	14. (a)	15. (a)	16. (a)	17. (b)	18. (a)	19. (c)	20. (b)
21. (a)	22. (a)	23. (d)	24. (a)	25. (d)	26. (a)	27. (c)	28. (a)	29. (d)	30. (d)

Chapter 05

1. (a)	2. (b)	3. (a)	4. (d)	5. (b)	6. (a)	7. (a)	8. (a)	9. (b)	10. (d)
11. (c)	12. (b)	13. (c)	14. (d)	15. (a)	16. (b)	17. (d)	18. (c)	19. (c)	20. (a)
21. (b)	22. (b)	23. (a)	24. (d)	25. (d)					

Chapter 06

1. (c)	2. (a)	3. (d)	4. (c)	5. (d)	6. (c)	7. (b)	8. (c)	9. (d)	10. (d)
11. (b)	12. (b)	13. (b)	14. (c)	15. (a)	16. (d)	17. (a)	18. (b)	19. (c)	20. (c)
21. (c)	22. (b)	23. (b)	24. (c)	25. (c)					

Chapter 07

1. (a)	2. (d)	3. (d)	4. (c)	5. (d)	6. (b)	7. (b)	8. (b)	9. (b)	10. (d)
11. (d)	12. (a)	13. (a)	14. (d)	15. (d)	16. (b)	17. (b)	18. (b)	19. (d)	20. (a)
21. (c)	22. (b)	23. (c)	24. (a)	25. (d)	26. (b)	27. (d)	28. (a)	29. (c)	30. (b)
31. (b)	32. (c)	33. (a)							

Chapter 08

1. (d)	**2.** (d)	**3.** (d)	**4.** (b)	**5.** (a)	**6.** (b)	**7.** (b)	**8.** (a)	**9.** (a)	**10.** (d)
11. (b)	**12.** (a)	**13.** (d)	**14.** (a)	**15.** (a)	**16.** (a)	**17.** (c)	**18.** (b)	**19.** (b)	**20.** (a)
21. (b)	**22.** (a)	**23.** (d)	**24.** (a)	**25.** (c)	**26.** (a)	**27.** (d)	**28.** (c)	**29.** (a)	**30.** (c)
31. (b)	**32.** (c)	**33.** (c)	**34.** (c)						

Chapter 09

1. (d)	**2.** (a)	**3.** (c)	**4.** (c)	**5.** (c)	**6.** (d)	**7.** (d)	**8.** (a)	**9.** (a)	**10.** (d)
11. (c)	**12.** (c)	**13.** (c)	**14.** (c)	**15.** (b)	**16.** (d)	**17.** (a)	**18.** (b)	**19.** (b)	**20.** (b)
21. (d)	**22.** (a)	**23.** (c)	**24.** (a)						

Chapter 10

1. (d)	**2.** (b)	**3.** (a)	**4.** (a)	**5.** (a)	**6.** (c)	**7.** (b)	**8.** (a)	**9.** (b)	**10.** (a)
11. (b)	**12.** (a)	**13.** (a)	**14.** (d)	**15.** (b)	**16.** (a)	**17.** (b)	**18.** (d)	**19.** (c)	**20.** (a)

Chapter 11

1. (b)	**2.** (c)	**3.** (a)	**4.** (b)	**5.** (d)	**6.** (b)	**7.** (d)	**8.** (b)	**9.** (c)	**10.** (c)
11 (d)	**12.** (b)	**13.** (b)	**14.** (a)	**15.** (b)	**16.** (c)	**17.** (b)	**18.** (c)	**19.** (c)	**20.** (c)
21. (b)	**22.** (a)	**23.** (b)	**24.** (d)	**25.** (a)	**26.** (a)	**27.** (d)	**28.** (d)	**29.** (a)	**30.** (c)
31. (d)	**32.** (c)								

Chapter 12

1. (a)	**2.** (d)	**3.** (b)	**4.** (d)	**5.** (a)	**6.** (a)	**7.** (c)	**8.** (d)	**9.** (c)	**10.** (a)
11. (d)	**12.** (d)	**13.** (d)	**14.** (c)	**15.** (b)	**16.** (b)	**17.** (c)	**18.** (d)	**19.** (d)	**20.** (a)
21. (d)	**22.** (a)	**23.** (b)	**24.** (d)	**25.** (d)	**26.** (d)	**27.** (d)	**28.** (c)	**29.** (c)	

Chapter 13

1. (c)	**2.** (b)	**3.** (b)	**4.** (d)	**5.** (c)	**6.** (d)	**7.** (d)	**8.** (d)	**9.** (c)	**10.** (c)
11. (c)	**12.** (b)	**13.** (c)	**14.** (c)	**15.** (b)	**16.** (b)	**17.** (c)	**18.** (d)	**19.** (c)	

Chapter 14

1. (c)	**2.** (b)	**3.** (c)	**4.** (a)	**5.** (c)	**6.** (a)	**7.** (a)	**8.** (c)	**9.** (d)	**10.** (c)
11. (a)	**12.** (b)	**13.** (b)	**14.** (a)	**15.** (a)	**16.** (b)	**17.** (b)	**18.** (b)	**19.** (d)	**20.** (d)
21. (b)	**22.** (d)	**23.** (b)	**24.** (a)	**25.** (c)	**26.** (a)				

Chapter 15

1. (a)	**2.** (c)	**3.** (d)	**4.** (b)	**5.** (c)	**6.** (a)	**7.** (c)	**8.** (b)	**9.** (c)	**10.** (b)
11. (c)	**12.** (c)	**13.** (a)	**14.** (c)	**15.** (d)	**16.** (a)	**17.** (d)	**18.** (b)	**19.** (b)	**20.** (c)
21. (a)	**22.** (a)	**23.** (a)	**24.** (c)	**25.** (b)	**26.** (b)				

Chapter 16

1. (a)	**2.** (d)	**3.** (c)	**4.** (a)	**5.** (c)	**6.** (a)	**7.** (a)	**8.** (b)	**9.** (d)	**10.** (a)
11. (d)	**12.** (b)	**13.** (a)	**14.** (c)	**15.** (b)	**16.** (a)	**17.** (b)	**18.** (a)	**19.** (a)	**20.** (a)
21. (c)									

Chapter 17

1. (b)	**2.** (b)	**3.** (b)	**4.** (a)	**5.** (d)	**6.** (c)	**7.** (b)	**8.** (b)	**9.** (a)	**10.** (d)
11. (a)	**12.** (d)	**13.** (c)	**14.** (a)	**15.** (b)	**16.** (d)	**17.** (c)			

Chapter 18

1. (d)	**2.** (a)	**3.** (a)	**4.** (b)	**5.** (b)	**6.** (d)	**7.** (c)	**8.** (d)	**9.** (a)	**10.** (d)
11. (b)	**12.** (d)	**13.** (a)	**14.** (b)	**15.** (c)	**16.** (b)	**17.** (d)	**18.** (d)	**19.** (b)	**20.** (b)
21. (c)									

Chapter 19

1. (a)	**2.** (b)	**3.** (a)	**4.** (b)	**5.** (c)	**6.** (b)	**7.** (d)	**8.** (c)	**9.** (b)	**10.** (d)
11. (c)	**12.** (d)	**13.** (d)	**14.** (d)	**15.** (a)	**16.** (a)	**17.** (d)	**18.** (d)	**19.** (d)	**20.** (a)
21. (d)	**22.** (b)	**23.** (b)	**24.** (b)	**25.** (a)	**26.** (a)	**27.** (a)	**28.** (c)	**29.** (d)	**30.** (d)

Chapter 20

1. (c)	**2.** (a)	**3.** (c)	**4.** (d)	**5.** (c)	**6.** (d)	**7.** (b)	**8.** (a)	**9.** (a)	**10.** (b)
11. (a)	**12.** (b)	**13.** (a)	**14.** (b)	**15.** (a)	**16.** (a)	**17.** (c)	**18.** (d)	**19.** (a)	**20.** (c)
21. (a)	**22.** (c)	**23.** (c)	**24.** (b)	**25.** (a)	**26.** (a)				

Chapter 21

1. (c)	**2.** (a)	**3.** (c)	**4.** (b)	**5.** (c)	**6.** (d)	**7.** (b)	**8.** (d)	**9.** (b)	**10.** (a)
11. (d)	**12.** (c)	**13.** (b)	**14.** (b)	**15.** (d)	**16.** (d)	**17.** (c)	**18.** (c)	**19.** (d)	**20.** (d)
21. (a)	**22.** (c)	**23.** (a)	**24.** (b)	**25.** (a)	**26.** (b)				

Chapter 22

1. (c)	**2.** (d)	**3.** (a)	**4.** (c)	**5.** (b)	**6.** (a)	**7.** (d)	**8.** (b)	**9.** (a)	**10.** (d)
11. (c)	**12.** (c)	**13.** (c)	**14.** (d)	**15.** (c)	**16.** (d)	**17.** (c)	**18.** (d)	**19.** (d)	**20.** (d)
21. (a)	**22.** (c)	**23.** (c)	**24.** (d)	**25.** (a)	**26.** (d)	**27.** (d)			

Chapter 23

1. (c)	**2.** (a)	**3.** (c)	**4.** (d)	**5.** (c)	**6.** (d)	**7.** (d)	**8.** (b)	**9.** (a)	**10.** (a)
11. (c)	**12.** (a)	**13.** (b)	**14.** (a)	**15.** (d)	**16.** (b)	**17.** (a)	**18.** (c)	**19.** (d)	**20.** (a)
21. (d)	**22.** (b)	**23.** (c)							

Chapter 24

1. (d)	**2.** (b)	**3.** (d)	**4.** (c)	**5.** (b)	**6.** (c)	**7.** (b)	**8.** (c)	**9.** (d)	**10.** (d)
11. (a)	**12.** (a)	**13.** (a)	**14.** (d)	**15.** (a)	**16.** (a)	**17.** (c)	**18.** (d)	**19.** (c)	**20.** (c)
21. (d)	**22.** (c)	**23.** (c)	**24.** (a)	**25.** (c)	**26.** (c)	**27.** (d)			

Chapter 25

1. (d)	**2.** (b)	**3.** (c)	**4.** (b)	**5.** (b)	**6.** (c)	**7.** (a)	**8.** (d)	**9.** (c)	**10.** (a)
11. (a)	**12.** (a)	**13.** (c)	**14.** (a)	**15.** (a)	**16.** (d)	**17.** (b)	**18.** (b)	**19.** (d)	**20.** (c)
21. (a)	**22.** (a)	**23.** (d)	**24.** (c)	**25.** (a)					

Chapter 26

1. (b)	**2.** (a)	**3.** (b)	**4.** (a)	**5.** (b)	**6.** (c)	**7.** (a)	**8.** (b)	**9.** (d)	**10.** (c)
11. (a)	**12.** (c)	**13.** (c)	**14.** (a)	**15.** (d)	**16.** (b)	**17.** (c)	**18.** (c)	**19.** (a)	**20.** (c)
21. (c)	**22.** (b)	**23.** (b)	**24.** (a)	**25.** (a)					

Chapter 27

1. (c)	**2.** (b)	**3.** (c)	**4.** (b)	**5.** (d)	**6.** (d)	**7.** (a)	**8.** (b)	**9.** (d)	**10.** (d)
11. (c)	**12.** (b)	**13.** (c)	**14.** (c)	**15.** (c)	**16.** (b)	**17.** (c)	**18.** (c)	**19.** (a)	**20.** (d)
21. (a)	**22.** (a)	**23.** (d)	**24.** (a)	**25.** (c)					

Chapter 28

1. (b)	**2.** (a)	**3.** (d)	**4.** (c)	**5.** (a)	**6.** (c)	**7.** (b)	**8.** (c)	**9.** (d)	**10.** (c)
11. (d)	**12.** (b)	**13.** (a)	**14.** (d)	**15.** (c)	**16.** (c)	**17.** (d)	**18.** (b)	**19.** (d)	**20.** (b)
21. (a)	**22.** (d)	**23.** (a)	**24.** (c)	**25.** (c)	**26.** (a)	**27.** (c)	**28.** (b)	**29.** (a)	**30.** (c)
31. (c)									

Practice Set 01

1. (d)	**2.** (b)	**3.** (b)	**4.** (b)	**5.** (c)	**6.** (d)	**7.** (b)	**8.** (a)	**9.** (b)	**10.** (a)
11. (d)	**12.** (a)	**13.** (a)	**14.** (c)	**15.** (a)	**16.** (d)	**17.** (a)	**18.** (b)	**19.** (c)	**20.** (b)
21. (a)	**22.** (c)	**23.** (a)	**24.** (c)	**25.** (b)	**26.** (a)	**27.** (c)	**28.** (a)	**29.** (c)	**30.** (d)
31. (a)	**32.** (a)	**33.** (c)	**34.** (b)	**35.** (a)	**36.** (b)	**37.** (b)	**38.** (a)	**39.** (c)	**40.** (b)
41. (a)	**42.** (b)	**43.** (b)	**44.** (a)	**45.** (b)	**46.** (b)	**47.** (a)	**48.** (b)	**49.** (b)	**50.** (a)

Practice Set 02

1. (d)	**2.** (b)	**3.** (a)	**4.** (c)	**5.** (d)	**6.** (d)	**7.** (b)	**8.** (a)	**9.** (b)	**10.** (b)
11. (b)	**12.** (b)	**13.** (d)	**14.** (c)	**15.** (b)	**16.** (d)	**17.** (b)	**18.** (a)	**19.** (d)	**20.** (b)
21. (a)	**22.** (c)	**23.** (a)	**24.** (c)	**25.** (d)	**26.** (a)	**27.** (c)	**28.** (a)	**29.** (c)	**30.** (a)
31. (d)	**32.** (d)	**33.** (c)	**34.** (b)	**35.** (a)	**36.** (c)	**37.** (d)	**38.** (c)	**39.** (c)	**40.** (b)
41. (b)	**42.** (a)	**43.** (a)	**44.** (a)	**45.** (a)	**46.** (a)	**47.** (c)	**48.** (a)	**49.** (c)	**50.** (b)